The coming
of the
Warrior-King

Zephaniah simply explained

Daniel Webber

EP BOOKS

(Evangelical Press) Unit C, Tomlinson Road, Leyland, England, PR25 2DY

www.epbooks.org
epbooks@100fthose.com

First published 2004

British Library Cataloguing in Publication Data available

ISBN 978-0-85234-556-6

In memory of
Robert J. Sheehan,
whose friendship and encouragement
originally prompted the writing of this book

Contents

Abbreviations and Bible versions .9

Preface. 11

Introduction (2 Chronicles 34). 15

Part 1: Setting the scene (1:1) 29

   1   The man, the message, the season
       (1:1 and 2 Kings 22:1–23:37) 31

Part 2: His coming in judgement (1:2–3:8) 43

   2   God will judge his world (1:2–3) 45

   3   God will judge his people (1:4–13). 55

   4   The great Day of the Lord (1:14–18) 73

   5   God's judgement is mixed with mercy (2:1–3) 87

6   God's judgement will extend
      to the nations (2:4–15) 103

7   God's judgement will embrace Jerusalem (3:1–8) 125

Part 3: His coming for restoration (3:9–20) 145

8   God will restore hope to all his people (3:9–13). .147

9   God will restore rejoicing among
      his people (3:14–17). 161

10   God will restore blessedness
      to his people (3:18–20) .179

Notes 195

Abbreviations and Bible versions

ASV   American Standard Version (1901)
AV (KJV) Authorized / King James Version (1611)
c.   circa, about (with dates)
cf.   compare
ESV   English Standard Version (2002)
Ibid.   Ibidem, in the same place (referring to previous entry in notes)
JB   The Jerusalem Bible (1968)
JM   James Moffatt's A New Translation of the Bible (1936)
NEB   New English Bible (1970)
NIV   New International Version (1979)
NKJV   New King James Version (1982)
RSV   Revised Standard Version (1952)

Preface

One of the greatest needs of the modern church is to know God and to know him better. Indeed, it is often suggested that what we actually need is a deeper experiential knowledge of God, and this is undoubtedly true. We need a knowledge of God that not only stimulates the mind, but moves the heart to worship and the will to obey. Nevertheless, a normal prerequisite to such blessing is a formal understanding of who God is and what he is like.

The most clear and certain source of such knowledge is, of course, to be found in the Bible. The books of both its Old and New Testaments furnish us with the kind of knowledge that is crucial to the life-changing discovery we wish to enjoy. However, if there is one part of that revelation that is more likely than others to be neglected it is that group of books collectively known as the Minor Prophets. And this is a pity. It is a pity because these books contain a rich vein of insight into the character of God. They also contain what some of us believe to be a necessary counter to the slight and superficial views of God which seem so prevalent at the present time. In contrast,

the particular prophecy under consideration in the book of
Zephaniah contains an awesome picture of the God who really
is, and whom we are all one day destined to meet. It also beckons
us—indeed, it pleads with us—to face up to what it will mean to
meet the living God.

The initial content of this commentary had its first outing
some considerable time ago. Prior to his sudden and unexpected
home-call in 1997, Robert Sheehan used to hold a 'Saturday
Seminary' for aspiring preachers, and those who simply wanted
to improve their understanding of the Scriptures. These
gatherings took place once a month in Welwyn and were a
means of instruction and blessing to a considerable number of
men. Although it was 'Bob' himself who did the lion's share of
the work, he was very good at roping other people in to help
with the teaching syllabus. I was one of those who was regularly
called upon in this way. One of the things he asked me to do was
to give a series of lectures on 'Preaching from the Old Testament
Prophets'. What we actually did was to look at general principles
for a couple of sessions and then to use Zephaniah's prophecy
as an expositional case study. A couple of years after Bob's death
I was asked to consider turning the work I had done in the
seminary into a brief commentary. When I finally began to turn
my mind to the task, I suddenly realized how much additional
work still needed to be done. Probably like most of the men
who have contributed to the Welwyn Commentary Series, I
have sometimes struggled to fit this work into an already over-
stretched schedule. Nevertheless, now that the book is finished,
I am most grateful for the experience that a more detailed study
of its content has provided. The volume itself I would like to
dedicate to the memory of the special friendship that I enjoyed
with the late Robert Sheehan.

It simply remains for me to thank those who, in different ways, have been particularly helpful in the preparation of this book. Firstly, everyone involved in the work of the European Missionary Fellowship is aware of the special debt of gratitude that they owe to the untiring labours of Joan McWilliams. She has been a faithful 'behind the scenes' worker for the EMF for more years than she probably cares to remember. Among her many duties, she is responsible for keeping my literary output on the grammatical 'straight and narrow' and I am grateful for this somewhat more public opportunity to acknowledge her input. Not only has she read this manuscript during its various stages of development, but she has made many helpful suggestions. Secondly, I am most grateful to the Lord for the provision of a very special 'help-meet'. Whatever small contribution I have been able to make to the work of the kingdom of God, I am sure that it could not have been done without the constant love and encouragement that Zurilia has so willingly and self-sacrificially given during more than thirty years. Finally, every would-be commentator and preacher is indebted to a vast array of people, both ancient and modern, who have travelled along the same road before him. A quick glance at the notes to be found at the end of this volume will soon reveal the names of my travelling companions.

Daniel Webber
Welwyn
March 2004

Introduction

Please read 2 Chronicles 34

Tucked away as it is among the Minor Prophets, and perhaps also because of its harrowing subject matter, Zephaniah is one of the most neglected books of the Old Testament. Rarely does it figure among those normally given priority treatment by the men in the pulpit or those who sit in the pews. This is not a criticism, merely an observation. From a purely natural point of view, who can really blame either the preachers or their hearers? After all, it might seem like a strange sort of individual who could be tempted to undertake a sustained expository treatment of a book which, for the most part, is almost unrelenting in its concentration on doom and gloom. In our somewhat superficial age, we possess neither the stomach nor the inclination for the kind of realism demanded by the contents of this prophecy.

But quite apart from the demands of the content, perhaps there are other reasons for this book's neglect. For example, it is possible that some would be put off by its historical setting.

All the immediate events of this prophecy are located during a period of Israel's history with which most people are at best only vaguely familiar. An additional problem could even be the style of literature with which we are confronted in this book. This is prophecy, and many would be somewhat wary about attempting to explain, let alone apply, this kind of material to their own day.

Therefore, in seeking to introduce readers to what may be unfamiliar territory, we must begin with a brief examination of the historical setting for Zephaniah's prophecy. Then we must turn our attention to a number of other background issues which, when explained, should make the message of this book a little more accessible.

The historical background
The opening verse of Zephaniah's prophecy identifies his ministry with the reign of Josiah, King of Judah (640–609 BC). This immediately places him between two important dates: the Fall of Samaria in 722 BC and the Fall of Jerusalem in 586 BC A general overview of this period is therefore important to our understanding of the message of this prophetic book.

1. Josiah's forerunners (715–640 BC)
Josiah's three most immediate forerunners were Hezekiah, Manasseh and Amon. By the time the first of these had ascended to the throne, the great days of a united monarchy under Saul, David and Solomon had already passed. In 931 BC a revolt of ten of the twelve tribes of Israel had divided the nation into two kingdoms. In the north, the kingdom of Israel was governed from its capital, Samaria, by Jeroboam (931–913 BC). In the south, the kingdom of Judah retained its links with the throne of David at Jerusalem. Idolatry and wickedness eventually led

to the downfall of Israel. In 722 BC Samaria capitulated to the Assyrians.

In contrast, the reign of Hezekiah (715–686 BC) was essentially characterized by faith. He earnestly sought to rid his kingdom of everything that might lead Judah to the same fate as her northern neighbour. However, with the accession of a new king, Judah was immediately plunged into the most appalling spiritual darkness. It is Manasseh (686–642 BC) who is held responsible for introducing prostitution and human sacrifice into the nation's worship (2 Kings 21:6-9; 2 Chronicles 33:6-9). In doing so, he sealed his nation's fate. God would not allow his people to sin with impunity and the Assyrians returned. As a captive in a foreign land Manasseh was brought to repentance and, on his eventual return to Jerusalem, he sought to undo the damage that he had previously done. Sadly, his attempts failed.

Manasseh was succeeded by his son Amon (642–640 BC), who reverted to the evil ways of his father. He was, however, only allowed to reign for two years before being assassinated by his servants (2 Kings 21:19-23; 2 Chronicles 33:20-24). These assassins were themselves executed and Josiah, Amon's eight-year-old son, took his father's place as king (2 Kings 21:24; 2 Chronicles 33:25).

2. Josiah's reign (640–609 BC)
Josiah's reign was distinguished by reformation. At the tender age of eight years, he was informed that his father had been murdered, the assassins executed, and that he was to be the new king. Although he was almost certainly influenced for good in matters of religion before this, by the time he was sixteen years old Scripture informs us that 'he began to seek the God of his father David' (2 Chronicles 34:3). Four years later he began to

purge Judah and Jerusalem of the pagan images which Manasseh had introduced during his reign (2 Chronicles 34:3–7). Indeed, he had even extended the influence of his reforms to the Assyrian-dominated northern kingdom (2 Chronicles 34:6–7).

It is possible that these reforms not only preceded the discovery of 'the Book of the Law of the LORD' in the temple (2 Chronicles 34:14–33), but also the ministries of both Zephaniah and Jeremiah (maybe by as much as six or seven years). If this timing of the initial reforms has been correctly interpreted, then it reveals a remarkable faith, courage and determination in one so young. After sixty years of contrary practice, it was no small thing to embark on such a reformation without prophetic backing. Nevertheless, in 622 BC—one hundred years after the Fall of Samaria—a copy of 'the Book of the Law of the LORD' was found, and with its discovery the reforms Josiah was seeking to implement suddenly took a dramatic leap forward. The powerful ministry of Zephaniah seems to have arisen at this point, supporting Josiah's reforms.

A series of attacks and counter-attacks between the Assyrians and Babylonians characterized the years between 622 BC and Josiah's death. In these clashes Egypt had aligned herself with Assyria. But even so, their combined strength was no match for the Babylonians. The great city of Nineveh fell in 612 BC and the rest of the Assyrian forces were defeated two years later at Harran (150 miles west of Nineveh). It was at this time, however, that Josiah made his fatal move. Having befriended the Babylonians, he intercepted the Egyptian army which was moving north in a vain attempt to lend assistance to the Assyrians. Josiah died at Megiddo in 609 BC (2 Chronicles 35:21–22).

3. Josiah's successors (609–586 BC)

Following Josiah's death, Judah plunged into rapid decline—a decline that was to end in the destruction of Jerusalem in 586 BC Initially, after a time of mourning, two sons and a grandson of Josiah took turns ruling Judah. Their failure to follow Josiah's godly reforms seems to indicate that Zephaniah's ministry had not only been appropriate, but necessary. Despite external appearances, resistance to Josiah's reforms had continued throughout his reign.

Perhaps in part due to the intervention of Josiah, Necho was unable to retake the city of Harran and was forced to return to Egypt. In the meantime, Jehoahaz had been appointed King of Judah (609 BC). But, on his way back to Egypt, Necho deposed Jehoahaz and made his older brother Eliakim (Jehoiakim, 608–598 BC) king in his place. Jehoahaz was taken to Egypt in chains. When Nebuchadnezzar first came to Jerusalem (605 BC) Jehoiakim's self-indulgent reign was already nearing its end. But by this time Babylonian dominance of the region was firmly established. Jehoiakim was replaced by Jehoiachin (598–597 BC) who, in turn, was replaced by Zedekiah (597–586 BC). Zephaniah had predicted Jerusalem's demise and the city finally fell in 586 BC

Further helps to understanding

Having placed Zephaniah's prophecy against the background of its historical setting, we must now turn our attention to other important issues which will aid us in our understanding of this book. The first two issues will focus on matters to do with the interpretation of the biblical text, while the remaining three will concentrate on issues relating to the book's content.

1. Rules of biblical interpretation

Given the fact that many sincere Christians have found themselves in all sorts of trouble as a result of inadequate interpretations of prophecy and prophetic books, two skills are vitally important. Firstly, we need a proper understanding of the general principles to be used in interpreting the Bible. Secondly, in order to avoid some of the pitfalls which can all too easily ensnare those with a penchant for prophecy, we must also seek to acquaint ourselves with a basic understanding of this particular genre.

A good preliminary guide to both disciplines is Wilfred Kuhrt's *Interpreting the Bible.*[1] Written with the mission-field in mind, it is a reliable introduction to this complex subject. As alternative introductions I would also recommend Richard Mayhue's *How to Interpret the Bible*[2] and *How to Read the Bible for All its Worth* by Gordon D. Fee and Douglas Stuart.[3] For those requiring something in more depth and detail, I would suggest either Louis Berkhof's *Principles of Biblical Interpretation*[4] or Patrick Fairbairn's nineteenth-century classic, *The Interpretation of Prophecy.*[5]

However, in focusing first of all on the most basic rules for the interpretation of Scripture, the summary provided by Bruce Milne in his *Know the Truth*[6] will be sufficient for our purposes. They are as follows:

Scripture is to be interpreted according to its literal sense
By this is meant that the most natural, straightforward sense of the words used is most likely to be the correct one. Here it is necessary to make a distinction between a 'literal' and a 'literalistic' approach in interpreting Scripture. The former view takes seriously the fact that the Bible is literature and

must therefore be interpreted according to the normal rules of grammar, speech, syntax and context; the latter does not. In applying this principle we must learn to ask the following questions: What did these words mean to those who originally received them? What kind of literature is being employed (prose, poetry, parable, allegory, hyperbole, etc.)? What circumstances form the context of the use of these words?

Scripture is to be interpreted by Scripture
This principle rests on a prior confidence in the Bible as the inspired Word of God and acknowledges that behind its many human authors this book is the work of a single divine mind. Therefore, not only can Scripture never contradict itself, but the reader is justified in, firstly, expecting a central theme to pervade the entire revelation of Scripture (i.e., salvation); secondly, looking to the clear statements on a given subject to be his guide in understanding the difficult; and, thirdly, interpreting the earlier parts of Scripture in the light of the later and fuller.

Scripture is to be interpreted under the guidance of the Holy Spirit
This principle intends to take seriously the Bible's own teaching on two important matters: firstly, that God has promised to give his Spirit to be our guide and teacher (John 16:13–15); secondly, that man's sinful nature obstructs his ability to truly understand and fully recognize the teaching of Scripture. Without the help and enabling of the Holy Spirit we are liable to shut out all evidence that is contrary to our own fallen prejudices and preferences.

Scripture is to be interpreted dynamically
Although Milne acknowledges that 'this final principle is really an extension of the third',7 it is meant to highlight the need for the Word of God to be properly applied to the present day. God's

Spirit is a living Spirit. It is partially with this in mind, and with a somewhat devotional concern, that I shall draw attention to what I have called 'Points to ponder' at the conclusion of each section of our exposition.

2. Understanding prophecy

The book of Zephaniah quite properly takes its place among the prophetic books of the Old Testament. But when we turn to such books, and the subject of prophecy, we need just as much care as when we are seeking to interpret Scripture generally. Indeed, we may need even more care. These books are sometimes the most difficult to read, understand and interpret in the entire Bible. Therefore, among the many pitfalls waiting to ensnare the unwary, two need particular attention: the first has to do with our expectations, and the second has to do with what Louis Berkhof calls 'the prophetic perspective'.

The difficulty relating to our expectations
Particularly among young Christians, it is often believed that the prophetic books of the Bible primarily address the future—especially the very end times. But this is a mistake. It is important to point out that it has been estimated that less than five per cent of the Old Testament's prophetic books describes the Messianic age, and that less than one per cent is devoted to events still to come.[8] Without wishing to go to the opposite extreme of suggesting that these books have nothing to say about the Messianic age or the end times, we do need to remember that the main targets of the Old Testament prophecies were the immediate people and circumstances of Israel, Judah and the surrounding nations.

Although we shall have more to say about this in the commentary itself, it is also important to realize at the very outset that prophets were essentially 'spokesmen', and their primary function was to speak for God to the times in which they lived. Probably the best way of thinking about these men and their task is to think of them first and foremost as 'forth-tellers', and only secondly as 'foretellers'. As it happens, both these aspects of an Old Testament prophet's ministry are found in Zephaniah's prophecy.

The difficulty related to 'the prophetic perspective'
When Berkhof somewhat disarmingly refers to what he calls 'the prophetic perspective', he is picking up on something that many commentators have observed. The term itself refers to the complex way in which prophecies that were meant to have a bearing on the historical circumstances in which they were set are also sometimes blended with, or set against the background of, a more distant and more significant eschatological future. Berkhof explains: 'The prophets compressed great events into a brief space of time, brought momentous movements close together in a temporal sense, and took them in at a single glance. This is called "the prophetic perspective" or, as Delitzsch calls it, "the foreshortening of the prophet's horizon". They looked upon the future as the traveller does upon a mountain range in the distance. He fancies that one mountain-top rides up right behind another, when in reality they are miles apart. Cf. the prophecies respecting the Day of the Lord, and the twofold coming of Christ.'9 Indeed, prophecies often give the impression of being fulfilled by instalments, with each fulfilment, until the last, being a pledge and a small foretaste of that which is to follow.

3. The theme of the book
Clearly the central theme of the book of Zephaniah is 'the Day of the Lord'. As we shall see in the exposition that is to follow,

in one way or another, direct reference to this occasion appears no less than eight times in the first chapter alone (1:7, 8, 9, 10, 14 (twice), 15, 18). In addition, the entire prophecy is set against the backdrop of this dominant, all-important day—this is true whether we are thinking in terms of an immediate judgement of the people of Judah, or the final destiny that awaits the entire world.

But it is not only 'the day' that is important to the message, but the one whose day it is. It is God's day. It is the Lord who will come in judgement and—perhaps, surprisingly, given the darkness of the picture that is set before us—in mercy. And what is this God like? He is awesome. It is essentially the Warrior-King who comes—proclaiming judgement, dispensing justice, avenging his broken covenant. He is 'the Lord of hosts' (2:9, NKJV) coming to do battle; he is 'the Mighty One' (3:17, NKJV), actively present among his people. For the most part the picture painted by this prophecy is so stark that the surprising feature is that there is room for mercy at all. However, there is salvation too, but it is hard won. Rebellious man must seek for it, and he must be earnest in his seeking (2:1–3). This must be his consuming passion, or he will be lost. He will fall under God's terrible wrath. In other words, there is no suggestion here of what, many centuries later, Dietrich Bonhoeffer would call 'cheap grace'.[10] Although important, it would not be enough for these people merely to change their creed; the whole direction of their lives must be changed. How could this come about? Again, we are back to the grace of God. The Lord will do something. But even from his point of view, grace is costly. Eventually it will cost him the death of his 'one and only Son', Jesus Christ. Therefore, throughout this book salvation is closely linked to judgement. It comes through judgement and, wonder of all wonders, it embraces both Jew and Gentile (3:9–10).

4. The timing of Zephaniah's prophecy

An issue that is not unimportant is the timing of Zephaniah's prophecy. This, in my view, is intimately linked to another point—namely, the prophet's use of, and dependence on, the content of the book of Deuteronomy (e.g., Zeph. 1:13; cf. Deuteronomy 28:30,39; Zeph. 1:16–17; cf. Deuteronomy 28:52). This suggests that the writer has recently been made familiar with the contents of the book of Deuteronomy and would place Zephaniah's ministry in a post-622 BC period. Such a timescale would provide an explanation for the dramatic reversal, following his death, of all the good that Josiah had achieved in his lifetime. According to this argument, opposition continued even after the discovery of the Book of the Law, with many simply restricting their conformity to outward observances (cf. Jeremiah 3:10). Conscious of the existence of this group, Zephaniah joins Josiah in warning of the inevitable consequences that would befall the nation. It is mainly this factor that leads me to favour the view that this prophet's ministry *followed* the discovery of the Book of the Law in 622 BC

Nevertheless, it has to be said that opinion among biblical scholars is almost equally divided on this matter. Indeed, if anything, the majority opinion among evangelical commentators is probably slightly in favour of Zephaniah's ministry starting before 622 BC It has to be admitted, however, that the evidence is not sufficiently conclusive for either side to claim certainty for their position. Furthermore, on whichever side of this divide an individual may fall, it need not significantly affect his understanding of the main theme of the book.

5. The absence of Messianic references

There is one other issue that has been of interest to commentators seeking to understand this book, and that is the virtual absence of any reference to the office of the Messiah. This factor Zephaniah shares with his prophetic contemporaries, Nahum and Habakkuk. The expectation of a king who would be a saviour of Israel was particularly developed during the eighth century BC with the prophecies of Hosea, Isaiah and Micah. So the question raised is: why is it that a century later this aspect of things has almost completely fallen out of the prophetic picture? The answer is probably related to two other factors: firstly, God's sovereign purposes for the nation; and, secondly, this people's misunderstanding of the nature of their relationship to him. The fact is that the fate of the nation had been sealed from the time of Manasseh. No amount of repentance could remove the stench of that period (cf. 2 Kings 21:10–15; 22:14–20).

Strangely enough, the people of Judah seemed to think that they and Jerusalem were inviolable. For them God had made promises concerning both the Davidic line and the city of Jerusalem and the idea that this could in any way be threatened was simply unthinkable. They thought they were safe for ever. Furthermore, in 701 BC the Assyrian king, Sennacherib, had laid siege to Jerusalem and the very fact that this assault on the city had collapsed and his death quickly followed seemed to confirm them in the conviction that, whatever happened, God was on their side. The prophets of this period, however, were fully aware of this fallacy and, very early on in his prophecy, Zephaniah makes it abundantly clear that God will judge their nation (1:9–12). It is also true that God would eventually provide a Saviour, but even this would only be accomplished by first creating a vacuum in Messianic expectation (3:9–20; especially vv.15, 17). At this time the main expectation and vision to be placed before their eyes was the fact that God would first come as a judge, and that he would judge *them*.

A summary outline of the book of Zephaniah

Having already given some indication above of the contents of the book, here we shall limit ourselves to a summary outline. As I have interpreted the book, it contains three parts.

First, there is the introduction, or what many commentators call 'the superscription' (1:1). This sets the scene for the entire book, speaking of the origins of the prophecy, the means by which its message was conveyed and the times in which it was delivered.

The second section is also the longest and, in many ways, the most demanding (1:2–3:8). It is an almost unrelenting announcement and description of a judgement that is to fall upon both the world and the ancient covenant people of God. The main focal point is on the latter, and we are told that the judgement will be terrible and certain. Nothing will halt it. Such has been the wickedness of the people that 'the Day of the Lord' will soon come and, when it comes, the people will wish that the mountains and the rocks would 'fall on us and hide us from the face of him who sits on the throne and from the wrath of the Lamb!' (Revelation 6:16)—except that here, of course, the message contains no reference to the 'Lamb'. Instead, it pictures a mighty warrior stepping forth to overwhelm his enemy.

After this the third section, though much shorter, is most welcome. It speaks of a glorious restoration (3:9–20). Not only does it point to a better gospel age, but beyond it to a new heaven and new earth. As the hymn-writer, Thomas Kelly (1769–1855), has reminded us:

Then we shall be where we would be;
Then we shall be what we should be;
That which is not now, nor could be,
Then shall be our own.

It simply remains for us to turn the pages and seek to get to grips with the message of this awesomely fascinating book.

Part 1:

Setting the scene (1:1)

1

The man, the message, the season

Please read Zephaniah 1:1 and 2 Kings 22:1–23:37

I n 1960 the playwright Robert Bolt completed what has now become a famous dramatic portrait of the sixteenth-century Roman Catholic humanist philosopher, Sir Thomas More. The title given to the play, which was subsequently made into an Oscar-winning film, was *A Man for All Seasons*.[1] The choice of both the character and the title seems to have been influenced by a concern to highlight this world's need for men of principle. In Thomas More, Bolt clearly believed that he had found such a man. Here, it is alleged, is a man who is willing to stand for that which he considers right, no matter what personal consequences may follow.

The basic storyline, at least according to Bolt, is well known. For a brief period between 1529-32 Thomas More the scholar was appointed Chancellor of England. Those were the days of an absolute monarch, and there were few who held such power as King Henry VIII. But Thomas More was someone who was prepared to defy even the wishes of Henry, and go to the scaffold, rather than sanction the king's divorce from Catherine of Aragon and remarriage to Anne Boleyn. Other complex issues were undoubtedly involved in this historical episode, but Bolt's primary contention is that, in Thomas More, sixteenth-century England had a man of outstanding principle, and this fickle world is always in need of such heroes.

Now whatever we may decide to be the rights and wrongs of the playwright's judgement on this particular individual, it is certainly true that Old Testament prophets were generally of this mould. They too were men of principle. As the Epistle to the Hebrews reminds us, among their number were those who were 'tortured ... faced jeers and flogging, while still others were chained and put in prison. They were stoned; they were sawn in two; they were put to death by the sword' (Hebrews 11:35–37). There was, however, an important distinction between them and the hero of Bolt's play. Those Old Testament heroes lived, suffered, and very often died, not simply as men of principle, but as mediators of the Word of God, a word that will 'endure for ever'. Indeed, it is because this is so, that these men and their messages will always be welcome among the true people of God.

With the opening verse of the book of Zephaniah we are brought face to face with *a man with a message for all seasons*—a man who spoke seriously and solemnly to his own day and who, because his message had a higher source of authority than even his own sincere heart and mind, continues to speak to every age. It will be our initial purpose to introduce this man and the message he delivered nearly 2,600 years ago. We shall want to know who he was, the nature of his task and the circumstances in which he lived—in other words, we shall need to acquaint ourselves with the man, his message and the season in which he conducted his ministry.

But, of course, any exposition cannot be allowed to end there; it must inspire us to enquire about the way in which this man and his message speaks to every age, including our own. Therefore, when this superscription is properly understood it will be seen to throw light on a number of important issues of continuing significance.

The man: who and what was he?

Our investigation of this important opening verse begins with the stated identity of God's chosen instrument on this occasion and the nature of the task he was called upon to perform.

1. His name

The first thing that we are told about this man is his name. It was 'Zephaniah'. Although it would probably be incorrect to attribute too much significance to the precise meaning of the name itself, we should at least note that his name means 'Hidden of the Lord'. Therefore, as many commentators have pointed out, it is possible that this could be a reference to his once having been the object of some special providential deliverance during a difficult period in his life, but this is by no means certain.

2. His royal ancestry

We are then informed that he was a man with a significant ancestral history. Like many of his kind, the sum total of our information about him is meagre, and yet this superscription does provide more of his genealogical details than is normally afforded an Old Testament prophet. We are informed that he was 'the son of Cushi, the son of Gedaliah, the son of Amariah, the son of Hezekiah'. It would seem that the main purpose of this information is to identify him as a descendant of Hezekiah, the fourteenth king of Judah, and to show that he was related to the king in whose reign he lived and ministered. In other words, he was of royal lineage.

3. His calling

Finally, we are introduced to the nature of his calling: he was a prophet of the one true and living God. We are justified in recognizing him as such by virtue of the book's opening words: 'The word of the LORD ... came to Zephaniah ...' This kind of statement is typical of one called to the prophetic office and is used elsewhere in the Old Testament in identifying such men (e.g., Jeremiah 1:1-2; Ezekiel 1:3; Hosea 1:1; Joel 1:1; Jonah 1:1; Micah 1:1; Haggai 1:1; Zechariah 1:1; Malachi 1:1). This designation is the most important thing about the man. He was a prophet. Prophets were, quite simply, messengers of God. They were called by God and entrusted with a particular task. If a man presumed to take this office upon himself, then he was regarded as a false prophet (Deuteronomy 18:20-22). A true prophet was a man who had responded to a divine call. As such his function was to stand between God and men and proclaim his Word. They were mediators of a message. Their role and function was to deliver what God had entrusted to them—nothing more, nothing less.

As mediators they were indispensable to the needs of the people. The main reason for this is simply explained. When speaking of God, theologians frequently remind us that he is 'Other'; that is, that the Creator of the universe is so holy, so separate from us, so transcendently above and beyond us that, if we are ever truly to know God, then he must take the initiative in making himself known to us. The Infinite and Holy One must stoop; he must condescend. Man cannot find God simply by relying on his own initiative. Furthermore, it is not merely man's finitude that forms a barrier to his knowledge of the infinite; it is also his sinfulness. By nature, like Adam, his instinct is to run and hide from God (Genesis 3:8). This view of man is in stark contrast to that of so many modern theorists who would have us believe that the world's religions represent man's long search for God. From a biblical point of view, the truth could not be more different. Although the world's religions may serve as a testimony to the existence within man of a sense of God's 'eternal power and divine nature', the religions themselves are an expression of man's determined flight from him (cf. Romans 1:18-32). Nevertheless, despite this, God condescends to make himself known, and the fullest and clearest way in which he has chosen to do so is by raising up servants specifically entrusted with the task of bringing his word to the people.

Whenever this happened it was considered a tremendous privilege, both for the messenger and the recipient of the message. For the messenger, the privilege lay in the fact that God had saved him, drawn him into his work and then made him an instrument for the dissemination of his will among the people. But it was also a tremendous privilege to be a recipient of the message, regardless of its precise content—whether it was an announcement of mercy or a warning of wrath. The fact remains that *God* had stooped to communicate, that the divine Sovereign had condescended to speak to a fallen world.

The message: what was he called upon to declare to the people?

When considering the message that the prophet was called upon to declare to the people, there are three points that need to be observed.

1. A message from God

Firstly, Zephaniah was to declare a message from God to the people. It is vitally important that we remember that although Zephaniah was given the solemn responsibility of delivering the message of this book to the people, he was not its ultimate author. He was an ambassador. He was God's chosen instrument; he was 'carried along by the Holy Spirit' (2 Peter 1:21). His great task was to set before the people 'the word of the LORD'.

2. A message of judgement

Secondly, the message that Zephaniah was called upon to deliver was primarily one of judgement. It was not entirely without hope, and in this respect his was typical of the messages that prophets were normally commanded to bring. Theirs was always a communication which combined the realities of judgement and mercy. Nevertheless, it was primarily a message of judgement that Zephaniah was to bring to the people of his day. The message was essentially this: that God would soon come to judge the people of Jerusalem and Judah for their sins. There would be no escape. Jerusalem would fall. It was a prophecy that was fulfilled in 586 BC when the Babylonian king, Nebuchadnezzar, finally defeated Judah, ransacked the temple and deported most of the nation's inhabitants to various parts of his empire.

3. An unwanted message

Thirdly, Zephaniah's message was one that the overwhelming majority of the people did not wish to receive. This too is the most frequent response of men and women to the Word of God. Not only did they not want to receive it; they were unwilling to believe it. 'After all,' they reasoned with themselves, 'we are the chosen people; we are the ones to whom the ancient promises have been delivered; surely God could not contradict himself and subject us to his wrath!' At the heart of this perspective was a terrible one-sidedness with respect to God's ancient promises. The people were only willing to recognize the promises of blessing that God had made to the faithful and obedient, but woefully overlooked his equally valid pledges to judge the faithless and disobedient (cf. Deuteronomy 28).

And the fact is that the nation of Judah was ripe for judgement. Despite the miraculous intervention of God in preserving the nation from the Assyrian threat during the days of Hezekiah, the people had still turned their backs on him, and had done so in the most dreadful manner. Not only had they given themselves to idolatry, but they had also introduced prostitution into their cultic rituals and sacrificed their children on the altar of Baal (2 Kings 21:6–9).

The season: when did Zephaniah live and minister as a prophet?

The final clause of this opening verse invites us to consider the precise timing of the prophet's ministry. He lived and ministered 'during the reign of Josiah son of Amon king of Judah'. These details immediately inform us of three things.

1. Days of reformation

Firstly, Zephaniah's ministry took place during days of reformation.[2] Josiah was the first godly king in Judah since Hezekiah. The latter had died in 686 BC and it was not until 640 BC that Josiah became king. Even then he was only eight years old and nearly sixty years had elapsed between his reign and that of his great-great-grandfather. As we have already observed, the intervening years had been characterized by the most appalling idolatry.

2. Days of discovery

Secondly, Zephaniah's ministry took place during days of discovery. We are informed that Josiah was sixteen years old when he 'began to seek the God of his father David' (2 Chronicles 34:3), and by the time he was twenty years old he had started to purge the nation of its idolatry. Then, in 622 BC (the one-hundredth anniversary of the Fall of Samaria!), when he was twenty-six years old, he discovered a copy of the law (the book of Deuteronomy). Appalled by what he read of the consequences that would befall a nation that had taken the path followed by Judah, Josiah humbled himself afresh before God. The Lord answered him by promising that the terrible judgement foretold in the law would not fall upon the people during his lifetime (2 Kings 22:1–20). But, far from encouraging complacency, this news simply served as a shot in the arm to the young king and his reformation. It was probably at this time, during the days immediately following the discovery of the Book of the Law, that Zephaniah's supporting ministry began.[3] He was to give support to Josiah's reforms. So far, so good. From this it might seem that these were advantageous days in which to carry out such a ministry. But all was not what it seemed.

3. Days of danger

Finally, Zephaniah's ministry also took place during days of constant danger. The fact that reformation had already commenced did not mean that the supporters of God and truth had things all their own way. Students of biblical history have often wondered why the reformation under Josiah did not survive his death. The answer may well be that there were still those in the country who preferred the former days—the less puritanical days—and longed for their return. They hated this king and his book. They hated this killjoy prophet and his message. And he, Zephaniah, even in such days, had to stand in the gap between God and men and, no matter what the outcome, proclaim his truth.

Points to ponder

As we turn from the opening introductory words of this prophecy, we need to ask ourselves the question: what do these words have to teach us today? Well, if we are allowed to fiddle with the order of our exposition and apply its message in a slightly different order, we would be justified in making four important observations.

1. It reminds us of one of the great needs of the church in the days in which we live.

As we shall see, the days in which we live are not so different from those of Josiah and Zephaniah. The nation in their day was in need of reformation—one that was spearheaded by a rediscovery of the Word of God. In our day the professing church of Jesus Christ is similarly in need of reformation. Certainly, in much of the Western world, we have been living off the blessings of a Christian heritage that is now in marked decline. Moreover, as the church has departed from its message, so society has slipped further and further away from God-honouring moorings. Therefore, what we need is a new reformation, a rediscovery of the timeless truths of the Word of God. This is something for which the church should be earnestly praying.

2. It teaches us something about the kind of men the church needs for such times.

We need men like Zephaniah. Of course, we cannot have prophets in the Old Testament sense, nor even like those that appeared in New Testament times. Such days have passed. The church has been built on the foundation of the apostles and prophets (Ephesians 2:20) and that foundation will never need to be relaid. But we still need men who are called by God— men who will faithfully stand in the gap and, with urgency and compassion, without thought of the cost to themselves, proclaim God's Word among his people, and to an unbelieving world. When it is obvious that such men are in short supply, the church should be earnestly beseeching the throne of grace that God would again raise up men of this ilk in her midst.

3. It reminds us of the need we have for men whose great concern will be to bring the Word of God to the people in such times.
We need men who will be faithful in bringing to the people 'the faith that was once for all entrusted to the saints' (Jude 3). In many modern churches men and women seem to be losing confidence in the authority of the Bible and the power of the Holy Spirit to effect a work through the preached word. Preachers too are often guilty of betraying the same lack of confidence. Men who once considered themselves preachers of the Word of God now seem happier in the roles of psychologist, magician, and/or entertainer. But what we need are men who are humble recipients of God's infallible Word and who are prepared to preach it 'in season and out of season' (2 Timothy 4:2).

4. It teaches us that we continue to be in need of the specific message of this book for our own times.
Zephaniah's message was 'a message for *all seasons*'. Although written some 2,600 years ago, and focusing on the somewhat unpalatable subject of judgement, this is a message desperately needed in our own day. As the church feels the increasing pressure of a secularized society to conform to its own material and temporal agenda, we are in need of a message that is going to focus minds on 'the Day of the Lord' and the need to prepare

for it. The world needs to hear this message too. Drunk as she is with her own rhetoric, which constantly assures her that this life is all there is, she needs to be reminded—whether she appears to be willing to listen or not—that a day is coming when every soul that has ever lived will stand before the judgement seat of Christ.

Part 2:

His coming in judgement (1:2–3:8)

2

God will judge his world

Please read Zephaniah 1:2-3

Old Testament prophets were often called upon to deliver a message about judgement. We ought not to imagine, however, that the appointed spokesmen normally found personal satisfaction in being conveyers of such tidings. For them the really important factor was that God had spoken, and the only appropriate response was for them to discharge their responsibility as faithfully as possible. Although not for commendable motives, in the prophet Jonah we do find an indication of the kind of tensions and sense of apprehension that must have filled at least some of these godly men. They were certainly not robots and there must have been times when they would have preferred not to have undertaken the task that was allotted to them.

Furthermore, unlike the simplistic outlook that too often prevails in modern Christian circles, these men knew that

faithfulness was no guarantee of immunity from either hardship
or death. Indeed, according to a Jewish tradition, death was
exactly the fate that finally overtook the prophet Isaiah in the
ministration of his sacred office. In *The Ascension of Isaiah* it is
said of this prophet of priestly lineage that, during the reign
of Manasseh (696–642 BC), he was placed inside the hollowed-
out trunk of a tree, and sawn in two.[1] It is possible that this
incident was uppermost in the mind of the writer of the Epistle
to the Hebrews when, in drawing to a conclusion his great list
of heroes, he spoke of those who 'were sawn in two' (Hebrews
11:37). To be an Old Testament prophet was, without doubt,
a potentially life-threatening occupation. Nevertheless, his
primary task was to be faithful in the discharge of his God-given
ministry, even when the primary focus of that message was likely
to make him the object of opposition.

Now it was such a ministry that was thrust upon the prophet
Zephaniah. Given its content, there can be little doubt that
the message he was called upon to deliver would have been
difficult to declare. Nevertheless, having set forth his credentials
as a prophet of the one true and living God (1:1), Zephaniah
immediately launches into the main theme of his prophecy. It is
a stunning announcement of judgement. It is a judgement that
is certain and terrible and will affect the entire world.

The certainty of judgement

The first thing to notice about this judgement of God is that it is
certain to occur. There are two realities that make this coming
judgement inevitable.

1. God himself announces it

Firstly, the judgement of God is certain because God himself
announces it. Twice, in verses 2 and 3, the very words of God

are placed in Zephaniah's mouth. Not only is there an initial announcement made—'I will sweep away everything from the face of the earth'—but this is itself immediately backed up by the words: '... declares the LORD'. In other words, these are not simply the words of a man. They carry all the weight and authority of one who cannot lie (Hebrews 6:18). If those who heard Zephaniah did not want to believe that what he said would come true, then let them beware. God is not the kind to promise and then fail to carry out his promises. His judgements are not like the idle threats which often pass from the lips of men. What he says he will do.

2. God himself will perform the deed

Secondly, the certainty of this judgement is confirmed by the assertion that it is God himself who will perform the deed. Secondary forces might be employed, but it is the arm of omnipotence that will truly perform the deed. The personal pronoun is employed four times in these two verses to indicate God's real and personal involvement in the judgement. Three times he says, 'I will sweep away ...' (1:2-3), and this is immediately followed by, 'I will cut off ...' (1:3, NKJV) This judgement is certain because God has not only declared that it will come, but that he will perform the deed. The Warrior-King is coming.

These are facts that ought to be taken into account by all who harbour suspicions that God's prophetic announcements will not be carried out. The awesome consistency of his revealed character ensures that 'Heaven and earth will pass away, but my words will never pass away' (Matthew 24:35). The Word of God is like the character of God; it is eternal and therefore can never fail (Psalm 119:89; Isaiah 40:8).

The severity of the judgement

Not only is this judgement certain but, when it comes, it will be severe. This is brought out in two different ways in the verses before us.

1. It will affect the entire world

God himself says that everything will be swept away:

> 'I will sweep away everything
>   from the face of the earth,'
> declares the LORD   (1:2).

These words contain an echo of those spoken to Noah prior to the great Flood. Having declared that it had grieved him that he had made man on the earth, God says to Noah, 'I will wipe mankind, whom I have created, from the face of the earth— men and animals, and creatures that move along the ground, and birds of the air—for I am grieved that I have made them' (Genesis 6:7).

Three times in the opening verses of Zephaniah's prophecy, the words translated 'sweep away' occur. And then, as if to emphasize the emphatic and comprehensive nature of the action to be undertaken, these words are followed by 'I will cut off' (1:3, NKJV). What needs to be done will be done, and everything will go! This aspect is further taken up with the announcement that this judgement will affect everything within the world: 'men and animals ... birds of the air and the fish of the sea' (1:3). The order in which this is stated suggests an undoing of the original creation, with the last being first and the first being last (cf. Genesis 1:20,21,24–25,26–28). In other words, everything in the creation will come under the judgement of God. Nothing will be spared.

2. It will particularly affect mankind

Nevertheless, in this whole process of judgement, it is man who is being singled out for special attention. *He* will be 'cut off ... from the face of the earth' (1:3). The distinction here seems to be that, whereas other *things* can be stumbling blocks, only *man* can be wicked: 'The wicked will have only heaps of rubble.' The meaning of the Hebrew word translated in the NIV as 'rubble' is somewhat disputed. Indeed, the NKJV translates the original as 'stumbling blocks' and, more obviously and immediately through its use of punctuation, links this word and its clause into the sentence which immediately precedes it. The sentence then reads as follows:

I will consume man and beast;
I will consume the birds of the heavens,
The fish of the sea,
And the stumbling blocks along with the wicked.

Another favoured translation of this same word is 'idols' [AV, NKJV margin]. Both translations quite naturally suggest the idea that sinful man has managed to twist everything in creation so as to serve his idolatrous purposes. However, no matter what the precise significance of this word may be, it is quite clear that man—even when he does not have biblical revelation to guide him—has a clear responsibility to live according to God's moral law, a law that is 'written on their hearts' (Romans 2:14-15). Therefore, because of his repeated failure—because of his persistent wickedness (as will be demonstrated throughout this prophecy)—judgement is not only certain to fall, but will be terrible when it comes. Here is a clear declaration: this is still God's world and, no matter what man may like to think to the contrary, it will always be ruled according to the dictates of his righteousness.

Two fundamental questions

The certainty and severity of the promised judgement of God
found in the opening lines of this prophecy raise two questions
of fundamental importance for an unbelieving world. Firstly,
does God have the right to do this? Secondly, does he possess the
power to carry it out?

1. Does God have the right to do this?

There are two ways in which the first of these two questions
can be profitably pursued: the first applies to the immediate
situation as it confronted both the world and the nation of
Israel during King Josiah's reign, and the second is certainly
pertinent to the general outlook of our own day. Taking these
two questions in order, we begin by asking, 'Is God justified in
making such an announcement? Does it not contradict promises
that he had previously made both to the world and to Israel?
For example, what about the promise made to Noah after the
universal flood? Did he not say, "Never again will I curse the
ground because of man, even though every inclination of his
heart is evil from childhood. And never again will I destroy all
living creatures, as I have done"?' (see Genesis 8:21). Indeed,
the words with which he commences this announcement of
judgement through the prophet Zephaniah extend far beyond
anything that was endured during the days of Noah. In this
further judgement God declares that not even the fish of the sea
will be spared.

   In part, the answer to this question is covered by the details
of the full extent of the covenant made with mankind through
Noah. Beyond the words to which we have already referred God
also said:

As long as the earth endures,
seedtime and harvest,
cold and heat,
summer and winter,
day and night
will never cease   (Genesis 8:22, emphasis added).

Not only does this remind us of the fact that God has never relinquished his right to judge the world that he has made, but also that the full severity of the judgement announced through Zephaniah may be deferred to a time beyond that which the prophet himself anticipated. It is generally believed that Zephaniah's prophecy of judgement found its initial fulfilment in the events of 586 BC, when Jerusalem was overthrown by the Babylonians. But even then, 'everything' was not consumed. This reminds us of that simple principle that must always be borne in mind when seeking to interpret prophecy—namely, that any one prophecy might contain within itself foretastes of events that still await a future dimension.[2] Furthermore, as far as the *enduring* element in the promises made to Israel is concerned, it was part of that nation's wilful mistake not to realize that God's promises through Moses were always conditional on their obedience, and that an ultimate fulfilment of all God's promises of everlasting blessing would only be realized through the mediatorial work of an equally promised Messiah—our Lord and Saviour Jesus Christ.

The second problem raised in connection with this announcement of judgement may be expressed in the following way: 'Isn't this announcement part of a well-known disparity between the Old and New Testaments? Have we not outgrown the God of the Old Testament? Hasn't this vengeful God of the Old Testament been superseded by the God of the New

Testament—the loving and merciful God and Father of our Lord and Saviour Jesus Christ?' But the simple answer is that it is the basic premise that is wrong here. When the text of Scripture is treated seriously, it is clearly seen that the God of the Old Testament is one who always mixes judgement with mercy, as does the God of the New Testament (cf. Psalm 103:7-14; Micah 7:18-20; John 3:16-18). The Bible is scrupulously consistent on this, as on other matters. What men and women of every generation have to face is the fact that the God of the Bible is the world's sovereign and righteous Creator and, as such, he demands righteousness from his subjects. These are factors which we are in constant danger of forgetting.

2. Does God have the ability to do this?
The second question, 'Does God have the power to effect the judgement he has announced?', is much easier to answer. Our answer must be in the affirmative. After all, he is the one who has called this universe into being from nothing. As the opening verse of the Bible says, 'In the beginning God created the heavens and the earth.' Furthermore, it is this same God who every moment holds everything together. He is 'sustaining all things by his powerful word' (Hebrews 1:3; cf. Acts 17:28; Colossians 1:17; 2 Peter 3:7), and rules sovereign over all (Romans 9:15-18; Ephesians 1:11; Revelation 4:11). It is the wilful opposition of unbelief that is generally responsible for calling this fact into doubt.

But the psalmist's response to such arrogance is: 'The One enthroned in heaven laughs; the Lord scoffs at them.' Indeed, he does more than this. He also 'rebukes them in his anger and terrifies them in his wrath' (Psalm 2:4,5). Not only does God have the power; he will also reveal that power in such an unmistakable fashion that all will know that he alone is God and there is none else. The Lord himself reminded the ancient patriarch, and (particularly) his wife, of this truth by means of a question which needed no verbalized response—he had only to ask, 'Is anything too hard for the LORD?' (Genesis 18:14; cf. Job 42:2; Jeremiah 32:17, 27; Matthew 19:26). If we have any idea of who the Lord is, we have no difficulty in answering the question.

Points to ponder

1. The final judgement of God is a reality that the world must one day face.
This is something that neither the church nor the world must be allowed to forget. No matter what their personal preferences might be, preachers must not neglect the public proclamation of the certainty of the coming wrath of God. It is the reality of this coming day of justice that alone makes sense of the injustice that not only exists, but very often seems to prevail, in this world. It is also the reality of this Day of Judgement that alone makes sense of the sacrificial death of Jesus Christ on the cross. Both the Old and New Testaments make sense of it in the only way possible: in his death, Jesus Christ bears the wrath that would otherwise fall on us. The prophet Isaiah speaks of the Suffering Servant as one who 'was pierced for our transgressions … crushed for our iniquities'. He goes on, 'The punishment that brought us peace was upon him, and by his wounds we are healed.' And then:

> We all, like sheep, have gone astray,
>   each of us has turned to his own way;
> and the LORD has laid on him
>   the iniquity of us all   (Isaiah 53:4-6).

Amazingly the same prophet announces that '… it was the

LORD's will to crush him and cause him to suffer' (Isaiah 53:10). And for what purpose? That he might bear 'the sin of many' (Isaiah 53:12). The same theme is taken up by the apostle Paul in the New Testament. Without equivocation he says, 'God made him who had no sin to be sin for us, so that in him we might become the righteousness of God' (2 Corinthians 5:21).

2. We need constantly to remind ourselves that this coming Day of Judgement is an absolute certainty.
No matter how much or how often it is dismissed or ridiculed, the people of God must not allow themselves to slip into a way of thinking or living which in itself is a practical denial of the reality of coming judgement. In the face of modern secularism we must ever remind ourselves that we are meant to think and live as those who are 'strangers and pilgrims' here, that we are passing through. To the degree that we live out our lives before a watching world in such a way as to deny these realities, so we contribute to the onlooker's confusion, arrogance and doom.

3. We need to remind ourselves that, when it comes, this judgement will be more terrible than anything we can possibly imagine.
Nothing can properly prepare us for such a day. No matter how much we read of it in the Scriptures, or in books that endeavour to expound its dreadfulness, we can be sure that the reality itself will almost completely surprise us. Perhaps, to some extent, that is how it should be. Nevertheless, our hearts need to be kept sensitive to the very real needs that will exist on that day. Moreover, the best way of remaining sensitive, without being totally overwhelmed, is to remember that there is a remedy, and that remedy is to be found in the one who 'loved me and gave himself for me' (Galatians 2:20).

God will judge his people

Please read Zephaniah 1:4–13

Although there is to be a final day when God will judge the entire world, the prophet Zephaniah wanted to make sure that the original recipients of his message clearly understood that there was to be a prior judgement, one that would begin with *them*—the inhabitants of Judah and Jerusalem, the people of God.

A stunning announcement (1:4,7)

This section begins with the words: 'I will stretch out my hand against Judah and against all who live in Jerusalem' (1:4). Focusing as it does on the favoured tribe of 'Judah' and the supposedly inviolable city of 'Jerusalem', this is a stunning announcement. When God speaks here of stretching out his hand, he clearly intends the people to understand that his power is to be unleashed against those he considers his antagonists. Similar terminology will be used later in this book in connection with Assyria (2:13). It is also used elsewhere with respect to Egypt (Exodus 3:20; Deuteronomy 4:32–34). But here—as on a previous occasion (Isaiah 5:25)—the antagonists against whom he will stretch out his hand in judgement are identified as his own people.

For the first time this judgement is identified as 'the day of the LORD' (1:7). In one way or another this designation will appear no less than five times before this chapter is complete. Its importance as a motif for the entire prophecy cannot be overstated. It is a description which is frequently used by Old Testament prophets to indicate a time when the Lord himself will come to take vengeance against the wicked. Occasionally this day is depicted as a day of deliverance (Isaiah 34:2–35:10), but it is always first and foremost a day of judgement (Amos 5:18–20).

In the section before us, Zephaniah introduces the idea of this day in a number of different ways. Not only is it 'the day of the LORD', but also 'the day of the LORD's sacrifice' (1:8). Further on it is simply identified as 'that day' (1:9,10), or as 'that time' (1:12). Principally it is, as we have already said, a day of terrible judgement; but it is also in some sense imminent. Indeed, the very first mention of this day emphasizes the fact of its close proximity: '... the day of the LORD is near' (1:7). This is meant to strike fear into the hearts of those who have rebelled against God. Yet, although it may not be immediately obvious, this is not only an invitation to fear, but to think, and to take appropriate action (2:1–3). Something terrible is about to happen, and the men and women of Judah ought to do something about it. But a clear note of urgency rings all through the message of this book. Men and women need to do something. God's judgement is coming, and it is coming against them. It is inevitable, and it is imminent. There is little prospect held out that any action on their part can turn aside his wrath, and it could arrive at any moment. Time is quickly running out for the people of Judah.

But why is this judgement coming at all? And why is it coming against them? Why are they being particularly singled out? The most basic answer to these questions is that they are singled out because of *who they are* and *what they have done*. The fact is, they are not just like everyone else. Not only have they been identified as the people of God and therefore recipients of innumerable blessings, but the privileges they have received make them particularly culpable for the sins they have committed. These facts require closer scrutiny.

They are a specially privileged people
All men and women are guilty of sin before God and therefore will be judged. But those who have enjoyed the special privilege of being set apart to be his own people are deemed even more guilty when they fail. This principle not only finds expression in the Old Testament; it is carried over into the New. When the writer of the Epistle to the Hebrews seeks to counter the dangerous possibility of apostasy among professing New Testament believers he begins by exhorting them to 'pay more ... attention ... to what we have heard'. The reason he gives is that '... if the message spoken by angels was binding, and every violation and disobedience received its just punishment [he is referring to the Mosaic revelation], how shall we escape if we ignore such a great salvation?' (Hebrews 2:1-3).

In one of the most chilling statements found in the New Testament, the same writer goes on to warn that if they persist with their sinful intentions they can only expect to face a fearful judgement 'that will consume the enemies of God'. He goes on to explain: 'Anyone who rejected the law of Moses died without mercy on the testimony of two or three witnesses. How much more severely do you think a man deserves to be punished who has trampled the Son of God under foot, who has treated as an unholy thing the blood of the covenant that sanctified him, and who has insulted the Spirit of grace? For we know him who said, "It is mine to avenge; I will repay," and again, "The Lord will judge his people." It is a dreadful thing to fall into the hands of the living God' (Hebrews 10:27, 28–31).

Returning to the situation as it affected their Old Testament counterparts, we need to remember that one of the reasons that judgement was to begin with them was simply that God had specially set them apart to be his people. Moreover, of all the tribes of ancient Israel, Judah had been the most privileged. And of all the cities that had been singled out for God's favour, none was more so than Jerusalem. Therefore, it was because the abuse of all their privileges was so evident that judgement was to fall on them.

This is always God's way of dealing with people. As the apostle Peter reminds us in his first epistle, '... it is time for judgement to begin with the family of God' (1 Peter 4:17). The principle upon which this works is quite simple: much will be required of those to whom much is given. Judgement is always apportioned commensurate with the privileges and opportunities given. Those given access to knowledge, positions of responsibility, leadership, etc.—whether in the world or in the church—are called upon to use their gifts wisely and well. Failure to do so not only threatens to bring judgement, but also places them in the front line of that judgement.

They are an extremely disobedient people

But there is a second reason for judgement to begin with Judah and Jerusalem. With privileges come responsibilities, and this ancient people had clearly abused their privileged status by disobedience. In this section (1:4–13) every sphere of the nation's life, and every kind and class of person, comes under God's scrutiny and condemnation.

1. The nation's worship (1:4–7)

First to come under the spotlight is the nation's worship. This has been characterized by idolatry of the worst kind. Baal-worship had been rampant since the days of Manasseh and Amon (cf. 2 Kings 21:1–9, 16, 21) and, even though a reformation had commenced, representatives of that former wickedness remained, waiting for a more convenient day. God's response is plain: 'I will cut off from this place every remnant of Baal, the names of the pagan and the idolatrous priests' (1:4). Every form of this worship was soon to be destroyed in the land. God has never been capable of accepting rivals. He is a jealous God (cf. Exodus 20:5; 34:14; Deuteronomy 4:24; 5:9; 6:15). Either Yahweh or Baal is God; no pluralistic approach to worship has ever been permitted by biblical religion. Moreover, its representatives too will be cut off. The same verb form that was used in verse 3 to describe what would happen to all creation is used again concerning these wicked priests: they will be 'cut off'. Indeed, so thorough will be this judgement that even their names will subsequently be forgotten.

Two things had combined to bring this judgement on the priests. Firstly, as priests they were supposed to provide and preserve a true way of access to the living God, but they had betrayed that trust. Secondly, the false way that they had offered in its place to needy, dependent souls contained some of the worst crimes committed by men among their fellows: the sacrifice of infants on the altar of Baal.

In his excellent commentary on the book of Zephaniah, Palmer Robertson helpfully comments: 'God established a priesthood to mediate oneness with his people. The very existence of priesthood implied weakness in humanity and a need for compassionate understanding in maintaining the way of access to God for the sinful. But under the corruptions of Baalism, the priesthood apparently offered the defenceless infant as a sacrifice. Instead of providing for the removal of sin, the priesthood instigated depravity of the worst sort.'[1]

Nevertheless, every vestige of this wicked religion is to be removed, along with all its representatives. The emphasis here is on the completeness of the judgement. Nothing will be left to remind the people of anything of this foul religion. God had established 'this place' (Judah and Jerusalem) as his dwelling place, but in the judgement that was soon to come, everything contrary to the purity that he required would be removed. In his *History of Redemption,* Jonathan Edwards comments that the judgement of the exile had the effect of terminating Israel's 'itch after idolatry'.[2]

But it was not only the worship of Baal that was a problem. There were 'those who bow down on the roofs to worship the starry host' (1:5). Some, having escaped the allurements of Baal-worship, had turned instead to other objects of worship such as the sun, moon and stars. This too was a form of worship common among both the Canaanites and the Assyrians and has its most obvious modern counterpart in those who daily consult horoscopes.

The Mosaic law had, of course, specifically warned against this form of idolatry. In Deuteronomy 4:19 we read, 'And when you look up to the sky and see the sun, the moon and the stars—all the heavenly array—do not be enticed into bowing down to them and worshipping things the LORD your God has apportioned to all the nations under heaven.'

However, instead of heeding this warning, these people were ascending to their rooftops in order to worship the created thing, rather than the Creator (Romans 1:25). Evidently, the practice of erecting altars on the rooftops of their houses had become commonplace (cf. 2 Kings 23:12; Jeremiah 19:13). It was probably motivated either by the simple desire to satisfy their need for externals in worship, or in order to be closer to their less than omniscient deities—perhaps to be seen by them!

Still others engaged in a form of syncretism and combined the worship of God with the worship of Molech. This is made abundantly clear from the next clause, which informs us that there were also 'those who bow down and swear by the LORD and who also swear by Molech' (1:5). To swear by any name—whether it be 'the Lord' or 'Molech'—is to acknowledge the authority of the one whose name is invoked. Molech is the name of an Ammonite god and is elsewhere repeatedly described as 'the detestable god of the Ammonites' (1 Kings 11:5, 7). Apart from the general fact that all idolatry is detestable to the Lord, what makes the worship of this deity particularly abhorrent is its demand that children be offered as sacrifices by fire.[3] The law of Moses demanded the death penalty for anyone who offered his child to Molech (Leviticus 18:21; 20:2-5). Nevertheless, King Ahaz burnt his children in the fire (2 Chronicles 28:3), and Manasseh did the same (2 Kings 21:6). It was this sin that was particularly cited as one of the main causes for the judgement that befell Samaria in 722 BC (2 Kings 17:17). It is an interesting fact that although Josiah destroyed the high places of Molech (2 Kings 23:10, 13), Ezekiel was still condemning this practice early in the sixth century BC (Ezekiel 16:20–22; 20:26, 31; 23:37). It was the exile that finally put an end to this form of worship, although it seems to have lingered on into the Christian era in North Africa among the Carthaginian Phoenicians.

Not only were there those who were willing to abandon themselves to false religion, and others seeking to combine truth with error, there were still others who were characterized by complacency and/or indifference in matters to do with the worship of God. These are described as 'those who turn back from following the LORD and neither seek the LORD nor enquire of him' (1:6). Only one class of individuals is referred to here. To turn one's back on God is the same as neither to seek nor enquire of him. It is not just idolatry that calls down the judgement of God upon us; religious indifference will do so too. To live *without* God in his world, but still to live *on* him, is a terrible crime. It is the worst form of parasitism. In the case of the inhabitants of Judah and Jerusalem there is an added obstinacy and wickedness, for they could not be excused on the ground of ignorance. If their former violations of God's law had been sins of commission, then this was the sin of omission. These people were guilty of practical atheism. It is a reminder to us that the proper worship of God requires conscious and directed effort.

So, having been blessed with the particular privileges devolved upon those designated the people of God, they had given themselves to paganism, syncretistic worship and practical atheism. They were meant to be a holy people, but they had disgraced themselves before the holy God. As a consequence,

God was ready to act: 'Be silent before the Sovereign Lord, for the day of the Lord is near' (1:7). This call to silence is a reminder that, no matter what their judgement of the situation may have been, they were still in the presence of the Holy One (Habakkuk 2:20; Zechariah 2:13; Psalm 46:10). Silence is the only appropriate response. The God of the covenant—the covenant they have abused—was coming, and getting closer every minute. It was the Lord of hosts, the Warrior-King, who was coming. And he was coming confident of a gloriously assured victory.

For Zephaniah, this day was not only near, but God had made all the necessary preparations for it: 'The Lord has prepared a sacrifice; he has consecrated those he has invited' (1:7). There is a touch of irony here. It was the Lord who would take the place of the wicked priests and the disobedient nation would be the sacrificial victim (cf. Isaiah 34:6; Jeremiah 46:10; Ezekiel 39:17–19). Such action ought not to surprise the people. After all, this is only what was foretold in the Mosaic covenant for those who proved to be disobedient. Moreover, God's wrath is particularly terrible where wrath has been spurned. What is not easy to determine is the identity of those whom the prophet refers to as the 'consecrated' ones whom God has invited. It could be a reference to the nations who will serve as God's instruments of wrath (Isaiah 10:5–10; Habakkuk 1:6); Jeremiah speaks in a similar way when the Babylonian, Nebuchadnezzar, is near (Jeremiah 34:18–20; cf. 7:33; 16:4; 19:7). However, it may, as some commentators suggest, simply refer to the wild birds and beasts of the field who sup at the table of covenantal condemnation. But no matter who or what is intended, there is no doubt as to why the people of Jerusalem and Judah are in trouble. Their idolatrous and indifferent attitude to the honour of God has brought them to this sorry state.

2. The nation's royal court (1:8–9)

But it was not just the nation's worship that was in trouble. The next sphere of life to come under the spotlight is that of the royal court. Rarely do ordinary people do that which they have not first seen among those who are supposed to be their leaders. And what do we find here? We discover that the nation's leaders have led the way in disloyalty to God:

> On the day of the LORD's sacrifice
>> I will punish the princes
>> and the king's sons'   (1:8).

Matthew Poole thinks that these are references to Josiah's sons and grandchildren and therefore an indication of what would happen between the reigns of Jehoahaz and Zedekiah.[4] But it seems more likely that Josiah's sons are implicated along with the rest of the nation's leaders. It needs remembering that, even before the discovery of the law, Josiah had managed to get himself married to two wives and had produced offspring from each of these marriages (2 Kings 23:31, 36). Some commentators suggest that a disenchantment with their father's religion could have stemmed from this root.

What is clear is that, as the one leading the reformation, the father was not directly implicated in the rebellion of his sons. On the contrary, Josiah was actively walking in the fear of the Lord, trying to implement the requirements of the law. Others within the royal court were, however, following a different path. Furthermore, it would seem that, not content with copying a foreign religion, their intoxication with foreign ways extended to customs of dress as well. It was a further sign of their religious disloyalty to the God of Israel. Therefore God's punishment was destined to fall on them and on 'all those clad in foreign clothes' (1:8).

Not content with aping the ways, dress and customs of an alien faith, they were intent on enriching themselves—even if this meant involving themselves in cruelty and dishonesty. Therefore, we read that 'On that day I will punish all who avoid stepping on the threshold' (1:9). Although Calvin thinks it 'too far-fetched', and prefers to interpret this clause as referring to the plundering of the houses of other people,5 it is probably best understood as a reference to a superstitious practice among the Philistines dating back to the time of the judges. Following what was from Israel's point of view a disastrous battle, the ark of the covenant had been captured by the Philistines. The captors then took their prized possession and placed it alongside the image of their god, Dagon, in their temple at Ashdod. However, when they awoke the next morning, they found Dagon prostrate before the ark of the covenant. They dutifully put the image back in its place and departed. But when they returned the following day, not only did they find that the image had fallen again, but this time its head and arms were broken off and 'lying on the threshold'. The narrator then makes the following comment: 'That is why to this day neither the priests of Dagon nor any others who enter Dagon's temple at Ashdod step on the threshold' (1 Samuel 5:5)—the idea being that Israel had adopted this practice.

If this interpretation is correct, then there is a touch of irony involved in the coupling of this clause together with the next: 'who fill the temple of their gods with violence and deceit' (1:9). Here are a people who are willing to take the trouble to observe the smallest details of a pagan custom, but are indifferent to the basic demands of God's law, which requires honesty and justice.

No one can properly complain when the Warrior-King comes in judgement. In the days of Noah, when 'the earth was corrupt in God's sight and was full of violence', God came and put an end to all but righteous Noah and his family (Genesis 6:11,13). Why should this generation imagine that it could be any different now?

3. The nation's commercial life (1:10–13)

The third sphere of life to come under the spotlight is the nation's commercial life. Even though we may be less than completely certain about such things, from the descriptions given it seems obvious that Zephaniah was very familiar with the layout of the ancient city of Jerusalem. He refers to 'the Fish Gate' and 'the New Quarter' (1:10), and he knows where 'the market district' (1:11) is situated. The 'Fish Gate' was important because this is almost certainly a reference to the main entrance to the city on the north side—the most likely place to be assaulted by an invading army. Owing to the existence of steep slopes on other sides of Jerusalem, this was the point at which the city was most vulnerable to attack. Although its precise location is uncertain, the 'New Quarter' could possibly be 'the Second Quarter' (AV, ASV, NEB) or 'the Second District' (NIV) identified in 2 Kings 22:14 (cf. 2 Chronicles 34:22). Zephaniah also speaks of 'the hills' (1:10), which may contain nothing more than a general description. But in the opinion of C. F. Keil this is a description of the hills surrounding the lower city.[6]

The main point, however, is that these were centres of trade and industry, and that devastation was to overtake them all. The reason was that covetousness and dishonesty lurked there. The prophet knew it; presumably the people knew it too. But God, who even knows the secrets of men's hearts, knew that there were many who had done very well at the expense of other people's poverty. They had grown inordinately wealthy and, at the same time, lazy and indifferent towards both God and men.

What, then, will happen as a consequence of this behaviour? The 'day' will come, and on that day there will be 'a cry' (or 'pleading'), 'wailing' and 'a loud crash' (1:10). In other words, no longer will the city be a place of refuge. Wherever the wicked turn, and wherever they may run, there will be no escape. Jerusalem will be engulfed in devastation. A sense of the utter despair of a people who have lost all hope is communicated through the crying and the wailing. It is a desperate scene. Some commentators have even suggested that the loud crash may refer to the sound of the idols, in whom they had foolishly placed their trust, being broken.

The greedy merchants are particularly singled out.

> Wail, you who live in the market district;
>> all your merchants will be wiped out,
>> all who trade with silver will be ruined   (1:11).

The once-thriving city will be brought to utter ruin. All those who had placed their security in their wealth—wealth gained through despicable means—will be reduced to ruins. No one will escape. These people had in the past survived many crises and had even begun to think that they could hoodwink God, to think that he could be morally indifferent to what they did. But their hidden assets would be discovered; their schemes would be unproductive and yield no satisfaction.

And just in case anyone should imagine that they could escape, the Lord depicts himself in the figure of an omniscient nightwatchman, sifting and searching, bringing judgement.

He says, 'At that time I will search Jerusalem with lamps' (1:12).
The picture is clear. The most thorough search is under way.
With lamp in hand, God sets out, determined to leave no place
undisturbed.

Just over a century earlier, the prophet Amos had similarly
spoken in God's name to an equally rebellious people. He had
said:

> I saw the Lord standing by the altar, and he said:
> 'Strike the tops of the pillars
>   so that the thresholds shake.
> Bring them down on the heads of all the people;
>   those who are left I will kill with the sword.
> Not one will get away,
>   none will escape.
> Though they dig down to the depths of the grave,
>   from there my hand will take them.
> Though they climb up to the heavens,
>   from there I will bring them down.
> Though they hide themselves on the top of Carmel,
>   there I will hunt them down and seize them.
> Though they hide from me at the bottom of the sea,
>   there I will command the serpent to bite them.
> Though they are driven into exile by their enemies,
>   there I will command the sword to slay them.
> I will fix my eyes upon them
>   for evil and not for good'   (Amos 9:1–4).

But, like that earlier kingdom, Judah has not listened and
therefore God will come 'and punish those who are complacent'.
It is the sin of omission that is now in view as the prophet

draws a word picture from the wine-making process in order to press home the reality of their utter indifference to God. They are those 'who are like wine left on its dregs' (cf. Jeremiah 48:11; Amos 6:1). Like the sediment of wine which settles and thickens if left undisturbed, the citizens have become settled in their indifference to God. Matthew Henry says that they have become 'intoxicated with their pleasures'.[7] Not only have they become indifferent, but they are depicted as those 'who think, "The LORD will do nothing, either good or bad"' (1:12). Although they may not be so bold as to say so with their lips, inwardly they have convinced themselves, either that they will go undetected, or that God is as indifferent to their behaviour as they are. It is a picture of abject apathy. But they could not be more wrong. The God who really exists is always actively involved in history. Moreover, as David Baker observes, their 'irresponsible theology is just as evil as outright revolt'.[8] In their case, however, their inadequate theology is combined with revolt.

Therefore, 'Their wealth will be plundered, their houses demolished' (1:13). Despite their disobedience and apathy, they think that God will do nothing. The concluding verse of this section underscores just how wrong they are. All that they most value—their material wealth, their strength and their power (for all are included)—will be taken from them. The blessings of the covenant (for that was ultimately what their wealth really consisted of) will be forfeited (Deuteronomy 8:17-18).

That is not all:

They will build houses
    but not live in them;
they will plant vineyards
    but not drink the wine   (1:13).

This is a sad picture of the most dire frustration. Even the curse that came upon Adam at the time of his fall in the Garden of Eden left him with the assurance that he would eat, albeit 'by the sweat of [his] brow' (Genesis 3:19). But even this is denied to those who are in breach of the covenant God had made with them (Deuteronomy 28:30, 39). And this loss and frustration constitute just a small part of that which was destined to come upon a privileged but disobedient people.

Points to ponder

There are several important points for us to consider in the light of the foregoing.

1. Although it is a tremendous privilege to be within the sphere of God's gracious provision, such privileges always bring responsibilities. This is so, no matter who or what we are, and no matter what gifts we have been given. We are all answerable for the use of the privileges and opportunities that have been bestowed upon us. This is true of the person who is simply living off the bounty of God's world, but without thought for the provider. This is true of the one who is within earshot of the message of the gospel, but who chooses to take no notice of it. This is also true of the Christian who, having received God's mercy, gives little thought, time, or attention to the need to convey its message to others. As our Lord himself has warned, 'From everyone who has been given much, much will be demanded; and from the one who has been entrusted with much, much more will be asked' (Luke 12:48).

2. Despite man's innate fallen tendency towards the choice of his own deity, the God of the Bible remains implacably opposed to the worship of any other supposed deity.
Idolatry, whatever its form, is opposed by him. This remains

as true today as it was when God announced from Sinai that 'You shall have no other gods before [or, "besides"] me' (Exodus 20:3; Deuteronomy 5:7). Moreover, it is not enough to argue that, because there is only one true God, man has the right to determine his identity, decide on the nature of his attributes, or calculate on the manner in which he is to be worshipped. God speaks for himself on such matters and it is vitally important that man learns 'to think his thoughts after him' on this as on any other matter.

3. It is an awesome fact that God's scrutiny and judgement extend to every area of life.
He is the Lord of every aspect of our lives. We cannot divide our lives between the sacred and the secular, imagining that in some way what we do in one sphere will compensate for what we do in the other. Every aspect of life is under the watchful eye of God. He is concerned about the way we worship, the way we govern our homes, churches and nation, the way we conduct ourselves in our work and play. God's scrutiny extends to 'every idle word' (Matthew 12:36; cf. Psalm 139; James 3). How awesome this is! Indeed, without the knowledge that there is one whose every moment was without reproach, there would be no hope for any of us. Therefore, how thankful we ought always to be for our Saviour's perfect righteousness and sacrificial death!

The great Day of the Lord

Please read Zephaniah 1:14–18

Without doubt the opening chapter of Zephaniah's prophecy is unrelenting in the pursuit of its main theme—the judgement of God. The darkest description of that wrath, however, is only now about to be given. Everything that has been said about it up to now has only been building towards this moment when, on the very brink of the abyss, a doomed nation is given a brief look over its edge and into *'the great day of the LORD'* (1:14). This is, of course, the same 'day' as that variously referred to earlier as 'the day of the LORD' (1:7), 'the day of the LORD's sacrifice' (1:8), and 'that day' (1:9–10). But there are two particular emphases that are brought to our attention in connection with this 'great day'. The first is that it will really come. Secondly, its arrival will be more awesomely terrible than they could possibly have imagined.

Reactions to this great day
When sinful men and women are faced with the prospect of
their own doom, they are liable to react with either fear or
unbelief.

1. Fear
Fear itself can result in one of two consequences. First of all, it
may simply result in *paralysis*. Overwhelmed with the prospect
of that which seems likely to overtake them, people become
incapable of doing anything. Head in hands, they slump into
their favourite armchair, bereft of any meaningful response.
The alternative reaction to the same experience may well be
the exact opposite of what we have just described. Fear may
well prompt another kind of person to *action*. When this is the
case, preparations are made in the hope that they may be able to
lessen the impact of the events deemed soon to fall upon them.
Such people may even harbour the thought that the doom,
whatever it may be, may still be averted.

2. Unbelief
But there is a second way in which men and women might
react to such news and that is to doubt whether the prophesied
doom will actually take place at all. In fact this is precisely
how many in Zephaniah's day did respond. They simply did
not believe that it would happen. To some extent this reaction
was understandable. After all, this world has rarely lacked
charlatans and/or madmen who have been only too willing to
make extravagant claims concerning the end of the world. And
it would seem that the overwhelming majority of those to whom
this message was delivered were simply unwilling to listen to
what they saw as an alarmist's prophecy of doom. It made little
difference to them that a man had appeared in their midst
claiming to represent the one true and living God, that 'the

word of the LORD' was upon his lips and that the needs of the people were desperately urgent. They would not be stirred. They would not listen. It made little difference to them that their history—even their comparatively recent history—was against their apathy. It made little impression upon them that the God whom their forefathers had known had regularly intervened in the affairs of the nation with deliverances and judgements. They even ignored the fact that much of the language used by this prophet was calculated to remind them of the most cataclysmic judgement that the world had ever known, Noah's flood, the remembrance of which was still embedded in every civilization. But they would not listen.

The reality of this great day

Therefore, twice in the opening sentence of verse 14, the reality of this day's coming is stressed. It 'is near—near and coming quickly'. In other words, not only is it 'near' (cf. 1:7), but rapidly getting nearer; indeed, it is much nearer than those to whom it was coming might have imagined.

1. An appropriate response

This should, of course, have been expected. Those whose hearts and minds were close to the details of God's law, as restated on the Plains of Moab, would have realized that the book of Deuteronomy had repeatedly made plain that sins like theirs would not be overlooked. They would be punished, and this punishment would not only be severe, but rapid in its execution (see Deuteronomy 4:23–26; 7:1–4; 11:16–17; 28:20).

One cannot help but think of the accumulative effect that the reading of this law, recently rediscovered, would have had on the mind of young King Josiah. Indeed, we are not left in any doubt about this. He immediately ordered his attendants to 'enquire of the LORD for me and for the people and for all Judah about what is written in this book that has been found' (2 Kings 22:11–13). The initial response that the king received to his enquiry simply confirmed his worst suspicions (2 Kings 22:16–17). There was, however, a morsel of comfort; because his response to the Word of God was to humble himself before the Lord, a stay of execution was promised (2 Kings 22:18–20).

2. No room for complacency

And so there was to be a delay; there was still time. But the people ought not to be deceived by this. The judgement would still come; there was no room for complacency. The king's humility had simply bought extra time. But the people should be in no doubt that judgement was still sure to come, and many of Zephaniah's contemporaries would witness it. Although they had no way of realizing it, even as these words were communicated back to the king, the nation was within thirty-six years of its coming. It is a sign of Josiah's genuine spirituality that, having received notice of a delay, he did not lapse into complacency himself. Indeed, the news he received acted as a further spur to reformation (cf. 2 Kings 23).

The reality of God's determination to judge a fallen world must never be allowed to be forgotten. The church's task is to keep this reality before the minds of men and women both inside and outside the church. It doesn't matter whether or not the church is ridiculed for doing so. The important thing is to keep a sense of this reality before those who would rather ignore or exclude it from their thinking. Just as every day brought this ancient nation closer to the Fall of Jerusalem in 586 BC, so the days of our own era are inexorably moving towards that ultimate 'great Day of the Lord'.

The awesome characteristics of this great day

But it is not just the nearness of this day that is set before us in these verses. We are also brought face to face with a glimpse of its awesome character. What sort of day will it be? What will that day be like? Mere words cannot fully convey the awfulness of that day—still less the one that will finally eclipse even that day at the world's end. Only when Nebuchadnezzar's army overran the ancient city of Jerusalem in 586 BC would its inhabitants understand the full import of the words that were being conveyed to them by Zephaniah. Likewise, it will only be on that day when every knee shall bow before the judgement seat of Christ that this world will finally realize the full import of this and subsequent warnings. But, in terms of the Old Testament, these words brought by Zephaniah are certainly among the most graphic descriptions of the sheer horror for some of 'the great Day of the Lord'.

In some ways this description is reminiscent of what took place at Mount Sinai just prior to, and immediately following, Moses' receiving of the Ten Commandments. There is the same sense of the dramatic; there is the same sense of terror among the people (Exodus 19:16-19; 20:18-19). But that is where the comparison ends. On that occasion the people had a mediator, in the person of Moses. Not so now. When the Day of the Lord comes, it will be more than trembling that will characterize the hearts and lives of those called upon to meet it. This is, first and foremost, 'a day of wrath' (1:15). In general terms that 'day' (mentioned seven times in two verses) will be one on which God's overflowing wrath will be poured out in vengeance, and none will be able to stand against it. God is enforcing the curses of his covenant. At this moment in time those destined to be on the receiving end of that day cannot be expected to take in the full sense of its awesome character. Nevertheless,

Zephaniah seeks to give some expression to what it will mean. The perspective that is given is largely that of the miserable recipient of God's wrath. The emphases are those of utter loss and abject terror.

So, when that day comes, what will it be like? In a series of dramatic statements, the prophet Zephaniah spells out some of its chief characteristics.

1. A day of bitter defeat (1:14)
Firstly, when that day comes, it will be a day of bitter defeat: 'Listen! The cry on the day of the LORD will be bitter, the shouting of the warrior there.' Or, as the NKJV renders the second clause, 'There the mighty men shall cry out.' All their once-boasted power and security is now seen for what it really is—utterly useless before the anger of the omnipotent God. Now all the people can do is to give utterance to the despair of one overwhelmed by a mightier Warrior.

2. A day without comfort (1:15)
Secondly, when that day comes, it will be a day without comfort: 'That day will be a day of wrath, a day of distress and anguish.' Clearly this is a description of utter emotional despair. Maybe a development is intended between the emotional despair of this first couplet and the physical in the second. For it will also be 'a day of trouble and ruin'. Just as there will be no comfort within, so, with the sight of the devastation meted out to the land before their eyes, there will be no comforts to be gleaned from their surroundings. Destruction and devastation will characterize the land on that day.

There is no relief in the third couplet of this verse, which probably emphasizes the terror of that day, for it will be 'a day of darkness and gloom'. Again, comparisons between this and an earlier day of blessing for the people of Israel cannot be forgotten. When the Lord was active in delivering his people from Egypt, one of the plagues sent against their enemies was that of 'a thick darkness', one that isolated and immobilized the inhabitants of the land (cf. Exodus 10:22). The fourth couplet speaks of 'a day of clouds and blackness'. This description is reminiscent of many places, in both the Old and New Testaments, in which God is awesomely present—and most prominently he is present in judgement. His presence is always a threat to the ungodly and at times the elements are made to reflect the seriousness of being in the presence of the Holy One (e.g., Deuteronomy 4:11; 2 Samuel 22:10; Psalm 97:2; Matthew 24:30).

3. A day without safety (1:16)
But very quickly another couplet is upon us. This time we are informed that, when that day comes, it will be a day without safety:

... a day of trumpet and battle cry
    against the fortified cities
    and against the corner towers.

The overall picture is most graphic: the Warrior-King has set out in battle, not only against the enemies of his people, but also against those who have once professed to be his own people. Why? Because they too are acting like his enemies. Like Jericho, the fortified cities will crumble. Every human defence against the Lord will crumble. As this terrible day unfolds, they will look in vain for a place of refuge.

4. A day without counsel (1:17)

Fourthly, when that day comes, it will be a day without counsel. God is here speaking personally and says, 'I will bring distress on the people and they will walk like blind men.'

This kind of distress is specifically mentioned as part of the curses of the covenant. In Deuteronomy 28:28–29 we read, 'The LORD will afflict you with madness, blindness and confusion of mind. At midday you will grope about like a blind man in the dark. You will be unsuccessful in everything you do; day after day you will be oppressed and robbed, with no one to rescue you.'

Moreover, this picture of the Lord smiting Israel with blindness finds a most dramatic fulfilment in Nebuchadnezzar's treatment of Zedekiah (2 Kings 25:6–7; cf. Isaiah 59:10; Lamentations 4:14; Acts 9:8). Commenting on the words, 'like blind men', Matthew Poole says that they 'shall neither know what to do nor where to flee, neither be fit for counsel nor action'.[1] In the midst of tribulation, sinners will perish without counsel or help. They will seek a way out of trouble without finding one. What a contrast this is to the promise of the gospel! With the coming of the kingdom of God blindness is exchanged for the most glorious light as 'the good news is preached to the poor' (Matthew 11:5; cf. 9:27–28; 12:22; 15:30–31; 20:30–34).

Once again, the question may be asked: why should all this trouble fall on this people? The answer is simply stated: 'because they have sinned against the LORD'. Here is the one consistently revealed reason for the judgement of God. In their case, of course, it is not merely sin that is the problem, but sin against the kindness of one who has made himself known and established a covenant with them. They have repaid his kindness with scorn. Having freely entered into this covenant, they have wilfully and dreadfully violated its terms. They are, therefore, without excuse and the curses of that same covenant are being brought against them. 'Their blood', they are told, 'will be poured out like dust and their entrails like filth.' One aspect of the heinousness of the people's wickedness, and the reason that they cannot expect to be forgiven, is located in that particular wickedness that was perpetrated during the reign of Manasseh— the shedding of innocent blood (cf. 2 Kings 24:4). According to the book of Numbers, 'Bloodshed pollutes the land'—the consequence being that '... atonement cannot be made for the land on which blood has been shed, except by the blood of the one who shed it' (Numbers 35:33). And so their blood will be shed. Indeed, their blood, even when shed, will prove of no more value than the dust, and their vital organs of no greater worth than dung. Although much blood will be shed when the great day comes—when Nebuchadnezzar's army arrives—it is not so much the quantity of blood-shedding that is emphasized, but the worthlessness of it.

5. A day without help (1:18)
Fifthly, when that day comes, there will be no help. The last verse of this section describes the utter helplessness of the people. It does so first of all by emphasizing the fact that nothing will be capable of saving them:

> Neither their silver nor their gold
> > will be able to save them
> > on the day of the LORD's wrath.

This refers to the customary way in which a threatened or defeated nation would seek to buy off its conqueror by offering a ransom. On this occasion such a ploy would not be possible. The

Lord is so set in his determination to pour out his wrath that this option is completely ruled out.

But perhaps there is still one other way in which they might seek to use their resources in order to escape the wrath to come. Perhaps they could use their wealth for the purposes of flight or concealment? This ploy too is sure to fail. Nothing can save them. The prophet continues:

> In the fire of his jealousy
>   the whole world will be consumed,
> for he will make a sudden end
>   of all who live in the earth.

Jealousy presupposes the existence of covenant love (cf. Exodus 34:14). This love has been seriously spurned and therefore there is no escape. Historically, Judah felt the full force of the Warrior-King's jealousy when the Babylonians arrived. Using the most descriptive language, the prophet Jeremiah is able to look back upon and record that which is prophesied here, but with this distinction: now the prophecy has been fulfilled. In the deeply disturbing book of Lamentations we read:

> In fierce anger he has cut off
>   every horn of Israel.
> He has withdrawn his right hand
>   at the approach of the enemy.
> He has burned in Jacob like a flaming fire
>   that consumes everything around it.
>
> Like an enemy he has strung his bow;
>   his right hand is ready.
> Like a foe he has slain

all who were pleasing to the eye;
he has poured out his wrath like fire
    on the tent of the Daughter of Zion   (Lamentations 2:3–4).

And, again, we read:

The Lord has given full vent to his wrath;
    he has poured out his fierce anger.
He kindled a fire in Zion
    that consumed her foundations   (Lamentations 4:11).

And yet this prophecy points beyond the immediate context of defeat for Judah and the Fall of Jerusalem at the hand of the Babylonians. This eighteenth verse brings us full circle, back to the point where the whole prophecy began and the reality of a universal judgement (1:2–3). God is still the Lord of the entire earth and, if judgement came to those privileged people, 'what will the outcome be for those who do not obey the gospel?' (1 Peter 4:17). The answer is clearly given: '... the whole world will be consumed' and '... he will make a sudden end of all who live in the earth.'

The first judgement points forward to the ultimate day when God will come and none shall be able to stand before him. This theme will be taken up and developed further when we get to the third chapter. But 'the day of God's wrath, when his righteous judgement will be revealed' (Romans 2:5), is as sure to come as the one that befell ancient Jerusalem. Then too there will be those who will call on the mountains and the rocks to 'Fall on us and hide us from the face of him who sits on the throne and from the wrath of the Lamb! For the great day of their wrath has come, and who can stand?' (Revelation 6:16–17).

Points to ponder

In considering the prospect of the coming of 'the great Day of the Lord' we can do little better in this section than to remind ourselves of the comments of the apostle Peter found in his second epistle.

1. The world has always been characterized by unbelief in relation to spiritual and eternal realities.

Peter wrote, 'First of all, you must understand that in the last days scoffers will come, scoffing and following their own evil desires. They will say, "Where is this 'coming' he promised? Ever since our fathers died, everything goes on as it has since the beginning of creation"' (2 Peter 3:3-4). This unbelief is nothing new. Each successive generation has revealed a sad consistency with respect to the reality of this day. But we should not be followers of them. Theirs is a 'wish fulfilment'; they believe what they want to believe. But unbelief will do nothing to prevent the eventual arrival of that day and, with it, the final appearance of the Warrior-King to overthrow his enemies.

2. As the Christian thinks about the great Day of the Lord, he must make sure that he is guided by the perspective supplied by God's written Word.

This is a far more reliable witness than the unreliable preferences of a world in rebellion against God. Again, speaking of the world, Peter states: 'But they deliberately forget that long ago by God's word the heavens existed and the earth was formed out of water and by water. By these waters also the world of that time was deluged and destroyed. By the same word the present heavens and earth are reserved for fire, being kept for the day of judgement and destruction of ungodly men' (2 Peter 3:5-7). Note that the world 'deliberately forget'. In other words, they know that what God has said is true, but they choose not to accept it (cf. Romans 1:18–23). What is it that they forget? They forget all that God has made known in his Word about the world's origins and therefore, by implication, their accountability. They also forget their history—that God has visited his world in judgement before, during the time of Noah. This same God—the God who cannot lie (Hebrews 6:16-18)—has pledged to keep this world together until that day when he will finally appear to judge ungodly men.

3. God's delay in bringing in this 'great day' is only a matter of our perspective.

'But do not forget this one thing, dear friends: With the Lord a day is like a thousand years, and a thousand years are like a day. The Lord is not slow in keeping his promise, as some understand slowness. He is patient with you, not wanting anyone to perish, but everyone to come to repentance' (2 Peter 3:8-9). This delay should in some sense be seen as a cause for celebration, and as a day of opportunity.

4. When the great Day of the Lord finally comes, it is likely to take most people by surprise.

'But the day of the Lord will come like a thief. The heavens will disappear with a roar; the elements will be destroyed by fire, and the earth and everything in it will be laid bare' (2 Peter 3:10).

5. The reality of the coming of the great Day of the Lord should be a spur to holy living.

'Since everything will be destroyed in this way, what kind of people ought you to be? You ought to live holy and godly lives as you look forward to the day of God and speed its coming. That day will bring about the destruction of the heavens by fire, and the elements will melt in the heat. But in keeping with his promise we are looking forward to a new heaven and a new earth, the home of righteousness' (2 Peter 3:11–13).

5

God's judgement is mixed with mercy

Please read Zephaniah 2:1–3

What are men and women to do when faced with the awful prospect of an abyss such as that which has been described in the first chapter of this prophecy? What was the ancient nation of Judah to do, faced as she was with the certainties of a coming judgement and the relentless hounding of one who seemed intent on her destruction? What can any of us do, confronted as we are with the twin realities of our own sinfulness and the inevitability of God's judgement— whether this judgement is set to coincide with our death, or the end of the world?

There is only one hope. It is that the one who has promised to visit the world in wrath might also provide a merciful shelter from its storm. It is precisely this kind of hope that the prophet Zephaniah now places before the people. But in order to find its safety, those who would avail themselves of its benefits must also do all that they can, while they can, to enter its harbour.

A historical likeness

A not too dissimilar choice was placed before an eighteenth-century congregation at Enfield, Connecticut, on 8 July 1741. It was on this day that Jonathan Edwards preached his (subsequently much-maligned) sermon, 'Sinners in the Hands of an Angry God'.[1] On the day in question the Great Awakening of 1740–42 had not reached this particular town. Indeed, the prevailing attitude in Enfield to the spiritual movement sweeping across the country was one of indifference. An eyewitness described the people as 'thoughtless and vain'.[2] But on the night before Edwards was due to preach, Christians in neighbouring towns had gathered in order to make the spiritual state of the people of that town a matter of earnest prayer. Their chief concern was that God, who was visiting many other places with gospel mercy and power, might not pass these people by.

That evening Edwards took as his text the words from Deuteronomy 32:35 (AV): 'Their foot shall slide in due time.' In a deeply disturbing, but eternally realistic appraisal, the preacher sought to remind his hearers that such was their sinfulness that the only thing that preserved them from slipping immediately into hell was the extraordinary patience and kindness of God. Against all natural expectations, that particular sermon had a profound effect upon its hearers. Another eyewitness, Eleazer Wheelock, observed that by the time the sermon had ended '... the assembly appeared deeply impressed and bowed down with an awful conviction of their sin and danger. There was such a breathing of distress and weeping, that the preacher was obliged to speak to the people and desire silence, that he might be heard.

This was the beginning of the same great and prevailing concern in that place, with which the colony in general was visited.'3

The circumstances confronting the people of Enfield, Connecticut, in the days of Jonathan Edwards were only superficially different from those facing Judah in 620 BC After all, 'the Day of the Lord' was coming, and all its horror would soon be upon them all. What could they do? Was there any hope? Would there be any shelter? Could they find mercy? As these few verses show, although the main emphasis is upon the difficulty of finding shelter, a genuine hope was being held out to those who would seek it. Nevertheless, great care must be taken so as not to interpret this hope of mercy in a way which suggests that 'the great day' itself will be turned back, or even delayed. The time has been set; it cannot be altered. What is now held out before the people is a ray of hope, an antidote to despair.

As Matthew Henry says, 'From first to last his design was, not to drive the people to despair, but to drive them to God and to their duty—not to frighten them out of their wits, but to frighten them out of their sins.'4

The reality of hope (2:1)
The previous chapter had concluded with the words:

> In the fire of his jealousy
>   the whole world will be consumed,
> for he will make a sudden end
>   of all who live in the earth   (1:18).

In view of this pronouncement, it might be suggested that the best thing that could be done was to scatter. Instead, chapter 2 opens with an admonition. Indeed, as many as five admonitions are made in the first three verses of the chapter. The amazing thing is that these admonitions are directed to a people who show no serious signs of being interested in their own welfare. Nevertheless, the Lord instructs them to 'Gather together, gather together ...'

On the background to these opening words, Palmer Robertson helpfully informs us that 'The first two words of this section build on the word *stubble* (*qaš*). As a verbal form, the root concept conveys the meaning of "gathering stubble". It is used with this meaning in passages describing the gathering of straw or stubble by the Israelites in Egypt (Exodus 5:7,12), the gathering of stubble on the sabbath (Numbers 15:32–33), and the widow's gathering of stubble in Elijah's day (1 Kings 17:10).'[5]

In other words, these words are used to convey the two things most necessary to the real welfare of the people of Judah at this time: a sense of their own unworthiness, and just a hint that there might still be hope for them. In their sinfulness they have reduced themselves to the likeness of mere stubble but, if they acknowledge their worthlessness by bunching themselves together, they might yet find mercy. What this required, of course, was the complete reversal of the self-confidence that still characterized so many within the nation. They must humble themselves before the Warrior-King in the hope that he might yet be merciful—or else they must suffer the consequences. Or, to take up the imagery suggested by Palmer Robertson, they must either humble themselves or expect to be gathered together like the stubble they have become—fit only to be burned (Malachi 4:1). They must humble themselves, or be humbled. This is their only hope. It still remains the only hope for all the peoples of the earth.

But this, according to most commentators, is precisely the problem. Judah is a nation that does not want to humble herself. This is why she is referred to in the way that she is: 'O shameful nation', or, as Palmer Robertson translates it, 'O nation that has no shame'. He goes on to say of this people that 'Not even a blush rises on its cheek from an awareness of its guilt before God.'[6] What was generally true of this nation as a whole was equally true of its individual inhabitants. Steeped in sin, they had become increasingly blind to it and, as all restraints are eventually thrown off, shame is hardly felt at all. When this happens, evil is called good, and good is thought evil. The nation may stand on the very brink of the abyss but, in her present state of mind, she seems prepared to plough on regardless.

The need to respond—quickly (2:2)

Something needs to be done, and it needs to be done quickly. Fortunately, the right man for the job is Zephaniah and he is on hand to call the people to repentance. There is an understandable note of urgency in his voice. He knows that these people must act, and they must act now. The danger they are facing is both urgent and imminent. He tells them, shameful though they are, that they must gather themselves together 'before ...' This is a key word. It is used three times in this one verse and its purpose is to reinforce the urgent need to do something before the moment of opportunity disappears.

1. *There is little time*

The one thing that the sinner must not do is to wait before humbling himself before God. He must not sit around looking for signs that the word of the prophet is going to come true. He simply doesn't have the time. He must act, and he must act now. He must do something 'before the appointed time arrives and that day sweeps on like chaff'. What a picture this is! The image used here is a familiar one for this sort of context (cf. Psalm 1:4; Isaiah 40:24; Jeremiah 13:24). God's awesome decree is fixed and cannot be altered, and there really isn't much time. Its outworkings will soon be upon them. The harvest has been gathered in; the sheaves are piled upon the floor. The workman arrives, digs his fork into the pile and tosses its contents into the air. As each piece ascends, wheat and chaff hang together for the last time. This solitary moment, before a gust of wind forces their separation for ever, is all the time that is left to this wicked and rebellious nation. They must act before it is too late.

2. There is fierce anger

Furthermore, action must be taken 'before the fierce anger of the LORD comes upon you'. What a terrifying figure 'the fierce anger of the LORD' presents! It occurs no less than thirty-three times in the Old Testament and rightly conjures up pictures of the most terrifying kind. Words cannot properly express what this can mean. Probably the nearest we can approach to anything like an adequate understanding of this picture is to compare it with the most extreme anger which is to be found in those who on earth wield the forces of a seemingly absolute power. But even this analogy is bound to break down, and for at least two reasons. Firstly, in human beings anger is normally associated with uncontrolled passion; such would never be true of God. Secondly, whatever image of fierceness we could concoct, somehow it would still need to be multiplied by infinity. For this is one of the most fearsome things about the anger of God: it is of a quality beyond anything that finite beings can imagine.

Nevertheless, in that sermon to which we have already referred—'Sinners in the Hands of an Angry God'—Jonathan Edwards sought to give meaning to at least one recognizable aspect of the fierceness of God's anger: it is *wrath without pity*.

He explains: 'When God beholds the ineffable extremity of your case, and sees your torment to be so vastly disproportioned to your strength, and sees how your poor soul is crushed, and sinks down, as it were, into an infinite gloom; he will have no compassion upon you, he will not forbear the executions of his wrath, or in the least lighten his hand; there shall be no moderation or mercy, nor will God then at all stay his rough wind; he will have no regard to your welfare, nor be at all careful lest you should suffer too much in any other sense, than only that you shall *not suffer beyond what strict justice requires.* Nothing shall be withheld, because it is so hard for you to bear.'7

Should we be tempted to respond with the suggestion that such words are beyond anything warranted by the teaching of Scripture, then Edwards has a justifying word at hand from the book of Ezekiel. Having been shown the awful idolatry still taking place in the temple at Jerusalem, Ezekiel hears this solemn prediction from the Lord. He says, 'Therefore will I also deal in fury; mine eye shall not spare, neither will I have pity: and though they cry in mine ears with a loud voice, yet will I not hear them' (Ezekiel 8:18, AV). We are reminded of the equally terrifying words that fell from the lips of the Lord Jesus Christ when, in the parable of the talents, he concludes with the words: '... throw that worthless servant outside, into the darkness, where there will be weeping and gnashing of teeth' (Matthew 25:30). Therefore, something must be done before this experience overtakes us.

3. There is endless wrath

But the prophet has not yet finished with his admonition. Again he presses his hearers to take action, but this time it is 'before the day of the LORD's wrath comes upon you'. There is only one difference between this and the previous clause, and it is that 'the fierce anger of the LORD' has become 'the day of the LORD's wrath'. It is a reminder of whose day, and whose wrath, it is that is coming.

It should come as no surprise that Edwards has something to say about this as well. He begins by reminding us that this is 'the wrath of an infinite God'. He then comments: 'If it were only the wrath of man, though it were of the most potent prince, it would be comparatively little to be regarded. The wrath of kings is very much dreaded, especially of absolute monarchs, who have the possessions and lives of their subjects wholly in their power, to be disposed of at their will ... The subject that very much enrages an arbitrary prince, is liable to suffer the most extreme torments that human art can invent, or human power can inflict. But the greatest earthly potentates, in their greatest majesty and strength, and when clothed in their greatest terrors, are but feeble, despicable worms of the dust, in comparison of the great and almighty Creator and King of heaven and earth. It is but little that they can do, when most enraged, and when they have exerted the utmost of their fury. All the kings of the earth, before God, are as grasshoppers; they are nothing, and less than nothing; both their love and their hatred is to be despised. The wrath of the great King of kings is as much more terrible than theirs, as his majesty is greater. Luke 12:4–5: "And I say unto you my friends, Be not afraid of them that kill the body, and after that have no more that they can do. But I will forewarn you whom ye shall fear: Fear him, which after he hath killed hath power to cast into hell; yea, I say unto you, Fear him."'[8]

And this wrath, remember, is everlasting. We refer to Edwards once more: 'It would be dreadful to suffer this fierceness and wrath of Almighty God one moment; but you must suffer it to all eternity. There will be no end to this exquisite horrible misery. When you look forward, you shall see a long forever, a boundless duration before you, which will swallow up your thoughts, and amaze your soul; and you will absolutely despair of ever having any deliverance, any end, any mitigation, any rest at all. You will know certainly that you must wear out long ages, millions of millions of ages, in wrestling and conflicting with this almighty merciless vengeance; and then when you have so done, when so many ages have actually been spent by you in this manner, you will know that all is but a point to what remains. So that your punishment will indeed be infinite. Oh who can express what the state of a soul in such circumstances is! All that we can possibly say about it gives but a very feeble, faint representation of it; it is inexpressible and inconceivable: for "who knows the power of God's anger?"'9

The proper character of our response (2:3)
So what is to be done in the face of such impending doom? There is only one reasonable, one meaningful, response.

1. Seek the Lord
They must make it their first priority to 'Seek the LORD'. Their only hope before this all-consuming and terrifying experience of the wrath of God is to be found in God himself. Three times Zephaniah urges the people to 'seek'. This had been their great failure before; they had neither sought nor enquired of the Lord (1:6). This is their only hope now. But there is to be nothing superficial about this seeking. It must be a genuine search. It must be wholehearted. It must be persistent (Jeremiah 29:13). It must be characterized by a penitent trust in the one they had previously abandoned.

2. Trust and obey
Only now does it become obvious that the prophet's hopes

are not so much with the 'shameful nation' at large, but with a smaller remnant. This theme will be developed more fully later on in the prophecy. But for now it is enough to know that there is a seeking remnant in the land and that they can be recognized by the characteristics of their response to their Lord. First of all, they are addressed by the words: 'all you humble of the land'. Humility is the undeniable evidence of the genuineness of their approach to God (Isaiah 66:2; James 4:6), but true humility always results in obedience and therefore they are further identified as those 'who do what he commands'.

Approximately 650 years later the apostle John would bring together the themes of trust and obedience in the following way: 'We know that we have come to know him if we obey his commands. The man who says, "I know him," but does not do what he commands is a liar, and the truth is not in him. But if anyone obeys his word, God's love is truly made complete in him. This is how we know we are in him: Whoever claims to live in him must walk as Jesus did' (1 John 2:3–6).

3. Righteousness and humility

But what is *this* remnant (from the people of ancient Judah) to do? Indeed, what are those to do who, even at this late hour, wish to join that remnant? Well, in addition to seeking the Lord—for all our hopes are to be found in him—they are to 'Seek righteousness, seek humility'. These admonitions are not, of course, intended to encourage the false notion of gaining salvation by means of one's own efforts. They are simply a further definition of what it means to 'seek the LORD'. They are to seek *from him* that which they do not possess of themselves. Interestingly, it was in similar terms that Amos had addressed the nation of Israel almost a century earlier when they were on the brink of a similar crisis. He proclaimed:

This is what the Lord says to the house of Israel:
'Seek me and live;
>do not seek Bethel,
do not go to Gilgal,
>do not journey to Beersheba.
For Gilgal will surely go into exile,
>and Bethel will be reduced to nothing.'
Seek the Lord and live,
>or he will sweep through the house of Joseph like a fire;
it will devour,
>and Bethel will have no one to quench it   (Amos 5:4–6).

And, again:

Seek good, not evil,
>that you may live.
Then the Lord God Almighty will be with you,
>just as you say he is   (Amos 5:14).

The twin graces of righteousness and humility are the key to a life lived earnestly before God (Matthew 6:33; James 4:6). So too is persistence. They are to go on seeking the Lord's face and favour and, as they do so, they are to be declaring their earnestness through lives of godliness and submission.

The single hope in response—'perhaps' (2:3)

Then what? Although the passage is not without its counterpart in the New Testament (cf. Acts 8:22; 17:27), this is where those of us who live in the fuller light of that later revelation might find some difficulty in understanding Zephaniah's tone. By way of encouragement he offers these people nothing more than a 'perhaps'—'*perhaps* you will be sheltered on the day of the LORD's anger'. The uncertainty which is implied in the use of the word 'perhaps' is intended to stress just how difficult it will be for anyone to find shelter on that terrible day. When the Babylonians come as the agents of God's wrath, both the righteous and the unrighteous will be caught up in the suffering. Both will be carried off into exile. Therefore, the only hope that is held out even to those who humble themselves before God and seek his ways is a 'perhaps'—perhaps they will be sheltered. There are no absolute guarantees on offer. All, even the very best, have broken God's laws. If any are spared it will ultimately be due to God's merciful kindness. The one thing that has never been on offer from God is 'cheap grace'. Even mercy is costly. The death of Jesus Christ upon the cross ought to make this abundantly plain.

1. What's the point?

In view of what has been said about the inevitability of the judgement soon to fall on this nation, it might seem superfluous to some to start seeking for mercy *now*. We can almost hear the scorning unbeliever retort: 'If what you have been saying is true, what's the use of doing anything? If we are lost, we are lost.' But this kind of logic is no match for the counsel of the eternal God. As the Puritan George Hutcheson once wrote, 'Though the Lord's eternal purposes are unalterable, yet his threatenings ... do include the exception of repentance.'[10]

The wisdom that is from above reasons like this: God has his hidden eternal purposes and these shall never be altered. But this same Lord has condescended to reveal part of his mind to a fallen world and, because there is a proper (though often mysterious) relationship between means and ends in the outworking of his purposes, we should choose to see in every command, admonition, warning and threat that he utters a possible lifeline to safety. Furthermore, we should reach out for this lifeline and, if possible, grasp it. Who knows—maybe what happened to ancient Nineveh may yet come to us? When the prophet Jonah finally arrived in that 'great city' his message was plain and uncompromising: 'Forty more days and Nineveh will be overturned' (Jonah 3:4). There seemed to be no hope. But what did the people do? This is what we read:

> The Ninevites believed God. They declared a fast, and all of them, from the greatest to the least, put on sackcloth.

> When the news reached the king of Nineveh, he rose from his throne, took off his royal robes, covered himself with sackcloth and sat down in the dust. Then he issued a proclamation in Nineveh:

> 'By the decree of the king and his nobles:

> Do not let any man or beast, herd or flock, taste anything; do not let them eat or drink. But let man and beast be covered with sackcloth. Let everyone call urgently on God. Let them give up their evil ways and their violence. *Who knows? God may yet relent and with compassion turn from his fierce anger so that we will not perish'*

> (Jonah 3:5–9, emphasis added).

And what happened? We then read these words: 'When God saw what they did and how they turned from their evil ways, he had compassion and did not bring upon them the destruction he had threatened' (Jonah 3:10).

2. What if there's no rescue?
'But', says the sceptic, 'what if God does not relent? What if there

is no rescue and the judgement still comes?' The 'wisdom that comes from above' remains undaunted. 'It does not matter,' it says. 'I will still have done the best thing that is open to me. I will have cast myself upon the mercy of God. There is nowhere else to go. He alone has "the words of eternal life" (John 6:68–69). And, finally, if I as a sinner fall under his wrath—well, I deserve no less. But who knows? I may yet find mercy. The everlasting arms may yet be stretched out to one who, like the dying thief (Luke 23:43), has found paradise at last.' Certainly the most foolish thing in the world for the sinner who is in the hands of an angry God to do is to ignore, or delay seeking, God's offer of shelter—even when, as in this case, there is little more than a hint that it might be granted.

Points to ponder

It is one of the great characteristics of Hebrew prophecy that, even when judgement is its most prominent theme, a door of hope is left open for those who will dare to walk through it. Messages of judgement are invariably mixed with promises of mercy. This is true of Zephaniah's prophecy too. This is, of course, what we should expect from a God who delights to show mercy (Micah 7:18) and has throughout history inspired hope among his people (Psalm 39:7; 71:5; Acts 24:15). It is important that we remind ourselves of such things. Even in this prophecy a window of hope is provided which beckons the needy to look through it.

1. These verses remind us that where there is life there is hope.
In Acts 17:28 the apostle Paul quotes from the sixth-century BC Greek poet Epimenides to the effect that '... in him we live and move and have our being.' The Greek poet was extolling the virtues of Zeus but, as far as the point Paul was making was concerned, it made little difference—except to his audience! He

could have quoted Old Testament writers to the same effect (Job 12:10; Daniel 5:23). As long as God still grants us the blessings of his common grace, there is hope both for us and for those we love. Those eternal fingers have not parted, and we have not simply been allowed to slip into the everlasting misery which is our just reward.

2. These verses remind us that where there is opportunity there is hope.
What a great blessing it is to be within reach of a faithful gospel ministry; to hear what many living round and about us, near and far, have so little prospect of knowing! It is one thing to have life, but it is quite another to be within sound of a prophetic voice. It is a great privilege to live in a country where the gospel can be regularly heard. It is a great privilege to find oneself in a gathering of God's people where there is the constant reminder of a heaven to be gained and a hell to be shunned. These are reasons enough for placing ourselves and others regularly under the ministry of the Word of God. It is all too easy for the world to get its grip upon our hearts, making them insensitive to these eternal realities. We ought also to do our best to keep our children within reach of the gospel for as long as is reasonably possible. If they are unconverted, but still hearing, there is hope that this precious Word, by God's Spirit, will properly set them seeking the Lord while they can.

3. These verses remind us that where there is encouragement there is hope.
When the soul begins to feel the realities of its lostness and unworthiness, it often requires very little encouragement to seek its own well-being. All it needs is the encouragement of a 'perhaps' and it is likely to follow the ray of light provided by that hope until it finds itself in the arms of the Saviour. Therefore,

those responsible for proclaiming the Word of God must make sure that hope is held out to those who are looking for it. In seeking to compensate for the modern tendency to play down the reality of God's judgement, we must not content ourselves with the proclamation of themes that leave little encouragement to seekers to go on with their search until they have found the Saviour. To speak of sin and death and judgement is a necessity, but it must never be the sum total of our gospel ministry. There must be an equal emphasis on the need for men and women to humble themselves before God, to seek, to turn and to live.

God's judgement will extend to the nations

Please read Zephaniah 2:4–15

What is God really like? It is not always easy to find a satisfactory answer to this kind of question. It is not that God has failed to make himself known. This, we are told, he has done, and in two particular ways.

First of all, there is what we refer to as *general revelation*. We mean by this that God has left adequate traces of his existence and power in all that he has made, and that this revelation is available to everyone. It is general in that the knowledge it yields is of a general sort—i.e., that God exists, that he is good, powerful, just, wise, etc.—and it is a revelation that is clearly available to all mankind.

Secondly, there is *special revelation.* This revelation 'does not negate, contradict, or supplant the content of general revelation, but goes beyond it, providing a crucial supplement to it. The Bible is the exemplar of special revelation. The Bible provides an enormous quantity of information about God which cannot be known from the study of nature alone.'[1] Supremely, special revelation unlocks the door to redemption for us. It reveals God as a God of redeeming love, as one who executes his purposes to save a fallen world through his eternal Son, Jesus Christ.

Slow to anger

But even though it is possible for man to have access to these sorts of revelation, the question with which we started this chapter, 'What is God really like?', remains existentially pertinent. In part this is because, even with all the information provided by general and special revelation, our knowledge of God will still fall short of the reality. We can know truly, but not completely. Furthermore, in the moment-by-moment of our existence, it is quite likely that particular aspects of God's revealed character will take centre stage in our thinking. This could so easily be the case when reading something like the book of Zephaniah. Superficially it seems to run on a single track. It is possible to emerge from its message with the conviction that God is primarily a God of justice, a God of judgement and wrath. He is, of course, characterized by these attributes; but he is so much more—and even this prophecy makes this plain. Not only is he a God of judgement; he is also a God of great compassion.

Indeed, it is possible to conclude that the God of the Bible is supremely a compassionate God. Drawing from the words recorded in Exodus 34:6, King David could remind himself of this comforting thought: 'But you, O Lord, are a compassionate and gracious God, slow to anger, abounding in love and faithfulness' (Psalm 86:15). Commentating on this statement,

John Calvin says, 'He is indeed no less worthy to be praised on account of his rigour, than on account of his mercy; but as it is our wilful obstinacy alone which makes him severe, compelling him, as it were, to punish us, the Scriptures, in representing him as by nature merciful and ready to forgive, teach us, that if he is at any time rigorous and severe, this is, as it were, accidental to him. I am speaking, it is true, in popular language, and such as is not strictly correct; but still, these terms by which the divine character is described amount in effect to this, that God is by nature so gracious and ready to forgive, that he seems to connive at our sins, delays the infliction of punishment, and never proceeds to execute vengeance unless compelled by our obstinate wickedness.'[2]

The prophet Ezekiel could go one step further than the psalmist and suggest that there is a certain reluctance in God to pour out his wrath; that he prefers mercy to judgement. Depicting 'the Sovereign LORD' earnestly pleading with those about to fall under his displeasure, he says, 'I take no pleasure in the death of the wicked, but rather that they turn from their ways and live. Turn! Turn from your evil ways! Why will you die, O house of Israel?' (Ezekiel 33:11).

An important connection
Something of this great compassion can be seen breaking through here in Zephaniah 2:4–15. Even though the passage primarily focuses on the judgement that will soon fall on Israel's neighbours, at least one aspect of its purpose is to draw the people of God through repentance into safety.

1. The Hebrew text
This is particularly evident in two ways: firstly, it is to be found in the Hebrew text of Zephaniah 2:4. Although not included as

part of the translation of the NIV, the Hebrew text of this verse begins with the word 'For' (i.e., *'For* Gaza will be abandoned ...'). The seventeenth-century commentator Matthew Poole believes that this connecting word simply informs us that 'there shall be no refuge for you among your neighbours'.3 I am persuaded, however, that it is an indication that the prophet is still expounding the theme of hope with which he started in verses 1–3. In other words, having called upon this 'shameful nation' to 'seek the LORD' (2:1–2), he now draws upon the foreordained destiny of the surrounding nations to provide an illustration of what will also happen to an impenitent Judah. This, in and of itself, is an act of great compassion. He has not simply left them to themselves. Not only does he warn them of a similar destiny to that which will overtake the unbelieving nations, but he uses it as an incentive for them to choose a different fate.

2. A moment of respite

Secondly, it is also possible to detect a hint of the same compassion in the sudden switch of emphasis from Judah to the surrounding nations. After all that has been said about the judgement of God against Judah and Jerusalem, he seems to be giving those people a brief period of respite. Using a similar rhetorical device to that employed by Amos one hundred years earlier, Zephaniah seems to be momentarily diverting their attention from something they would have found difficult to accept (God's judgement of them) to something they would have no difficulty at all in accepting (God's judgement of their enemies). Perhaps he is concerned to gain a hearing with a view to persuading his own people to repent. There will, of course, be a sting in the tail (*see* 3:1–8), but for the moment they are diverted. Moreover, the diversion holds out the prospect of blessings being devolved upon them at the expense of their enemies (2:6-7, 9). Could this possibly be another incentive, a means to lure the people to their safety?

So what does Zephaniah, and his God, have to say about the surrounding nations? It is clear that they will fall under the judgement of God. Whatever else this may say to Judah about their own situation, it is a clear indication that God's sovereign purposes extend to all peoples and that they are morally accountable for their actions too.

To the west: Philistia (2:4-7)
The first of the four prophecies of judgement announced against the surrounding nations focuses on Philistia.

1. Identification
The process of her identification begins with the naming of four of her principal cities: 'Gaza', 'Ashkelon', 'Ashdod' and 'Ekron' (2:4). An interesting omission from this list is Gath, the once-famous home of Goliath (1 Samuel 17:4). Together with Ashdod and Ekron, Gath briefly played host to the ark of the covenant and was included with the four cities mentioned on that occasion as being among those obliged to pay tribute to Israel (1 Samuel 5; 6:17). Perhaps the simple reason for Gath's exclusion now is that she is already subject to Judah's control. Apart from pinpointing the exact location of God's judgement, the only other possible point of interest in the listing of these names is that they are presented in a certain geographical order. The list begins with Gaza, the most southerly city, the remainder being cited in the order they would be met by someone travelling in a northerly direction along Philistia's coastline.

But it is not only the mention of these cities that identifies these people. They are also specifically named as the 'Kerethite people', and as those 'who live by the sea' in 'Canaan, land of the Philistines' (2:5–6). Their designation as 'Kerethites' is generally thought to be a reference to much earlier links with Crete (or Caphtor; cf. Amos 9:7). It is, however, as the Philistines that they are best known. Living on the western extremity of the land once promised to Israel (Exodus 23:31; Numbers 13:29; 34:6; Deuteronomy 3:27; Joshua 1:4), the Philistines are particularly known for their opposition during the time when Israel was seeking to establish its own monarchy. Referring to the specific mention of 'Canaan', Matthew Poole suggests that this is a reference to 'that part that the Philistines did by force keep from the Jews'.[4]

2. Devastation

In addition to the identification of this nation, the description given of these four cities combines to present an overall picture of total devastation:

> Gaza will be abandoned
>   and Ashkelon left in ruins.
> At midday Ashdod will be emptied
>   and Ekron will be uprooted   (2:4).

The one peculiar feature contained in this picture is that Ashdod is singled out as suffering its fate 'at midday'. There is considerable disagreement about the significance of this statement among the commentators. Some believe that it refers to the suddenness of the attack, taking place during a time of great vulnerability—the time of the siesta! Others think that it is a general reference to the length of time it took for their enemies to complete their work of destruction—half a day. The most likely explanation views these words as drawing attention to the absolute superiority of the forces that were pitched against the inhabitants of Ashdod. So superior were these forces that they had no need to employ the element of surprise that might have been afforded by either an early-morning or late-evening attack. So certain were they of victory that they could attack in broad daylight and confidently expect to overwhelm these cities.

But what will become of these cities? Verse 5 opens with an ominous 'Woe'. It will not be long before the same pronouncement is made concerning Jerusalem (3:1). But that is still in the future. At the moment another nation is in God's sights, and with good reason:

Woe to you who live by the sea,
    O Kerethite people;
the word of the Lord is against you,
    O Canaan, land of the Philistines   (2:5).

Nothing worse than this can be imagined. This God is not some mere local deity, the creation of stubborn and rebellious hearts. He is 'the Judge of all the earth' (Genesis 18:25) and he has weighed this nation in the balances too, and they have been found wanting. He says, 'I will destroy you, and none will be left' (2:5). It is not the land that will be destroyed, but the people who formerly dwelt in it. The land itself will be put to good, though different, use. 'The land by the sea, where the Kerethites dwell, will be a place for shepherds and sheep pens' (2:6). This once-flourishing commercial centre, a favourite trade route connecting three territories, would be turned into open pasture land. Others—not the Kerethites—would reap the benefit of their loss.

3. Forfeiture

The land would be turned over to their former enemies: 'It will belong to the remnant of the house of Judah; there they will find pasture' (2:7). The very use of this word 'remnant' should inspire hope in those who wish to be numbered among the true people of God. It means that although judgement will come, something will survive its devastation. Judgement is not annihilation; something will be left. For those who in dark and desperate days heed the warnings of God's Word, and who 'seek the Lord' in the way he has appointed, something is added to the 'perhaps' of an earlier verse (2:3).

Here is a new motive for repentance; the hint of a future salvation. In language reminiscent of the blessings promised to the people of Israel prior to their original entry into the promised land (Deuteronomy 19:1), a remnant is promised:

> In the evening they will lie down
>> in the houses of Ashkelon.
> The LORD their God will care for them;
>> he will restore their fortunes   (2:7).

Nothing will threaten their security—neither wild beasts, nor marauding bands. The last clause is capable of more than one reading. The NKJV prefers, 'And return their captives'—in which case it could even refer to the physical return of exiles. The NIV rendering suggests a more general restoration of fortunes (cf. Job 42:10).

This idea of a future restoration is at the heart of the promise made in the book of Deuteronomy, where we read, 'When all these blessings and curses I have set before you come upon you and you take them to heart wherever the LORD your God disperses you among the nations, and when you and your children return to the LORD your God and obey him with all your heart and with all your soul according to everything I command you today, then the LORD your God will restore your fortunes and have compassion on you and gather you again from all the nations where he scattered you' (Deuteronomy 30:1-3).

The key question, however, is whether Judah will learn from the Lord's treatment of her neighbours to the west. This is not a mere warning to the Israelites that the Philistines too will come under the judgement of God. It is an invitation to repent, and a renewed warning of the certainty of the fate that will overtake them should they refuse—warnings repeatedly given in the law (Deuteronomy 8:19-20; 28:58-65). As he did of old, so again the Lord sets before his people the choice of 'life and death, blessings and curses'. But he is not indifferent about the choice they will make. He urges them to choose life and blessing over death and curses: 'Now choose life, so that you and your children may live and that you may love the LORD your God, listen to his voice, and hold fast to him' (Deuteronomy 30:19-20).

To the east: Moab and Ammon (2:8-11)

From the Philistines in the west, attention now turns to Moab and Ammon to the east. There are, however, several new dimensions to this pronouncement. Firstly, God is now addressing Israel's blood relatives. Secondly, unlike the earlier announcement, the remnant are now depicted as actively participating in the spoiling of their enemies. Thirdly, the true worship of God is now anticipated throughout the earth. Suddenly salvation begins to play as significant a role as devastation.

1. Blood relatives

This oracle begins in the first person. God is speaking directly to two nations, both with close ancestral ties to the people of God. He says:

> I have heard the insults of Moab
>   and the taunts of the Ammonites,
> who insulted my people
>   and made threats against their land   (2:8).

Moab and Ammon were situated in a region that was once the scene of a most devastating outpouring of wrath. Indeed, the names of the cities of Sodom and Gomorrah have become bywords for wickedness and judgement. In patriarchal times these cities were guilty of the most odious crimes against God and man, and they justly suffered for it (Genesis 18:20–21). In connection with that terrible situation Abraham had approached God with the words: 'Will not the Judge of all the earth do right?' (Genesis 18:25). He did—by pouring out his righteous anger upon the inhabitants of these cities.

At that time Abraham's nephew, Lot, was living in Sodom. Although he and members of his family escaped the city's destruction, they had not entirely escaped its corruption. The nations of Moab and Ammon were subsequently to spring from an incestuous relationship between Lot and his daughters (Genesis 19:30–38). This was the beginning of the blood relationship between Israel, on the one hand, and Moab and Ammon, on the other. For this reason the people of God were both warned against, and restrained themselves from, opposing these peoples (Deuteronomy 2:9,19; Judges 11:14–28). Sadly, neither of these nations seemed willing to show the same consideration to Israel. Despite repeated prophetic warnings of the consequences of their actions, Moab and Ammon were constant thorns in the side of God's people (cf. Isaiah 15:1–16:14; 25:10; Jeremiah 9:26; 25:21; 27:3; 49:1–6; Ezekiel 21:20; 25:1–11; Amos 1:13–15; 2:1–3). But Israel's forbearance would serve to aggravate their culpability before God.

Insults, taunts and threats against 'my people' and 'their land' (2:8) are the specific reasons given for God's judgement against these nations. Elsewhere both Isaiah and Jeremiah would draw particular attention to the conceited arrogance of Moab (Isaiah 16:6; Jeremiah 48:29–30)—an arrogance that would eventually lead to her downfall. That day was about to come. For her part, Ammon had been relentless in seeking to undermine and shame Israel (1 Samuel 11:1–2; 2 Samuel 10:1–4; Nehemiah 4:3; cf. 2:10, 19; 4:7; Jeremiah 40:14). She had also violated the borders set for her by God and, in the process, ripped open 'the pregnant women of Gilead' (Amos 1:13). How could she possibly imagine that she would escape the judgement of God?

The fact is, neither nation will escape. So as to show how certain this is, God takes an oath: '"Therefore, as surely as I live," declares the LORD Almighty, the God of Israel ...' (2:9). The opening clause of this sentence is simply terrifying. In one awesome statement God brings together the kind of ingredients that would indicate that these nations were most certainly lost. Firstly, he swears by his own life. With two possible exceptions (Isaiah 49:18; Ezekiel 33:11), virtually every use of the clause 'as surely as I live' is used in connection with a curse. Secondly, he emphasizes his nature as the divine Warrior. He is all-powerful; he is 'the LORD of hosts'. Who can possibly imagine that they can withstand omnipotence? Thirdly, he identifies himself with the very people that the Moabites and Ammonites have persistently opposed. The apostle Paul might say to the Romans, 'If God is for us, who can be against us?' For these nations these words have been turned around to say, 'If God is against us, who can possibly help us?' The answer is: 'No one.'

As if to underscore this solemn fact, the oracle continues with the words: 'surely Moab will become like Sodom, the Ammonites like Gomorrah …' And what does this mean? Simply that their fate would be the same as that of those once-despotic cities, and each would become 'a place of weeds and salt pits, a wasteland for ever' (2:9). Situated, as they were, in the very region where those ancient cities had fallen, the use of this kind of imagery could not be more vivid.

For the Israelites themselves, there are echoes here of the curses also pronounced in the book of Deuteronomy on those who were disloyal to the covenant. In Deuteronomy 29:23 we read, 'The whole land will be a burning waste of salt and sulphur—nothing planted, nothing sprouting, no vegetation growing on it. It will be like the destruction of Sodom and Gomorrah, Admah and Zeboiim, which the LORD overthrew in fierce anger.' Indeed, what happened to Sodom and Gomorrah has repeatedly been used in Scripture to serve as a type of God's final judgement on sinners (Genesis 18:20; cf. Isaiah 1:9; Amos 4:11; Matthew 10:15; 2 Peter 2:6).

2. Spoiling their enemies

But, as was said earlier, one of the differences between the judgement brought against the Philistines and the one brought against these two nations is that the remnant of God's people will participate in the spoiling of their enemies. Once again attention is being drawn to a 'remnant'—a theme that is growing in importance. Here we are informed that 'The remnant of my people will plunder them; the survivors of my nation will inherit their land' (2:9). Not only is this an act of judgement, but part of the fulfilment of a promise made by God to Abraham. During his own lifetime, Abraham had magnanimously surrendered this land to Lot and his descendants. Nevertheless, it was destined to revert back to the rightful heir and his descendants (Genesis 13:8–15).

In verses 10 and 11 it is the voice of the prophet Zephaniah that comes back into prominence. His words are essentially a summary of what has just gone before. Not that his words are simply a repetition; there are two additional elements which require our particular attention here.

Firstly, we are given an insight into *the root cause for the judgement of these nations*. The book of Proverbs reminds us that 'Pride goes before destruction, a haughty spirit before a fall' (Proverbs 16:18) and this is the underlying problem afflicting Moab and Ammon. The prophet declares: 'This is what they will get in return for their pride, for insulting and mocking the people of the LORD Almighty' (2:10). Pride is, of course, the underlying problem of all sin. 'The old serpent spits his venom,' says Matthew Henry, 'and pride is at the bottom of it.'[5] Pride had been a distinctively obvious characteristic of Moab through the centuries (Isaiah 16:6; Jeremiah 48:29). Indeed, it had been repeatedly evident in both Moabite and Ammonite opposition to Israel (e.g., Numbers 22–25; Judges 10–11), and it is now cited as the cause of their downfall. This is a solemn reminder, if one was necessary, that to oppose God's people is to set yourself against God himself. He is not indifferent to the plight of his people, nor to the pride that spawns such opposition.

Therefore, 'The LORD will be awesome to them when he destroys all the gods of the land' (2:11). This reference to the awesomeness of God's presence among the people, destroying all the gods of Moab and Ammon, is almost certainly drawn from similar words found in the book of Deuteronomy. As a wilderness nation they had stood on the brink of the promised land, with hearts torn between anxiety and anticipation, and the God of the covenant had encouraged them forward with the following words: 'Do not be terrified by them [the nations they were about to engage in battle], for the LORD your God, who is among you, is a great and awesome God. The LORD your God will drive out those nations before you ...' (Deuteronomy 7:21–22). A little later a further encouragement against doubt and fear is given as they are reminded that 'the LORD your God is God of gods and Lord of lords, the great God, mighty and awesome ...' (Deuteronomy 10:17). So here too, not only is there an assertion of terror that awaits the Lord's overthrow of these proud nations and their deities, but comfort for the remnant who are on the right side of the Almighty's power. As a consequence they have no need to fear these nations.

3. Worldwide salvation

Secondly, and somewhat remarkably, in this part of the oracle we are also informed that *worship will be offered to God from all the nations of the earth*: 'The nations on every shore will worship him, every one in its own land' (2:11). Following the devastation of both Judah and the nations, the Lord's supremacy will be acknowledged by all the peoples of the world. Moreover, unlike the normal portrayal among the prophets of the nations making their way to God *via Jerusalem* (Isaiah 2:3), Zephaniah describes this worship as being offered by 'every one in its own land'. Of course, this was not the first time that such a perspective had been brought before the minds of the peoples of the Old Testament. Isaiah anticipated such a thing in the eighth century BC (Isaiah 19:19, 21, 23), Malachi makes a similar prediction two hundred years after Zephaniah (Malachi 1:11), and these are not alone among the Old Testament prophets in doing so. But what is remarkable in this prophecy is that such an event should be anticipated in the midst of such dark prophecies concerning the future of these nations. A significant fulfilment of this prophecy can now be identified with the coming of the gospel age of the New Testament, with Jesus Christ himself encouraging such an expectation (John 4:21–23). Nevertheless, even though this expectation will find increasing fulfilment prior to Christ's return (Matthew 24:14), its final completion will have to await 'a new heaven and a new earth' (2 Peter 3:13; Revelation 21:1–4).

In the meantime, the question that Judah needs to face is this: will she heed the warning presented by the fall of these nations? Will she 'seek the LORD while he may be found; [and] call on him while he is near'? (Isaiah 55:6).

To the south: Cush (2:12)

The shortest statement in this list of prophecies is reserved for Cush. The Lord himself is again the direct spokesman and he says, 'You too, O Cushites, will be slain by my sword.' The Cushites are to be identified as the remote Ethiopians, possibly the most southerly people known to the Hebrews. It is probably the remoteness of this nation that makes them the most perfect example to set before the people of God. If even the wicked in Ethiopia are not safe from the judgement of God, what hope is there for a disobedient covenant people?

But why is the statement about the Cushites so brief? It has been suggested that it is intended to highlight the immediacy of that nation's devastation; no sooner is it identified than it is destroyed. Whether or not this is so, the language used is most certainly intended to indicate God's direct involvement in bringing the judgement. It is his sword, wielded by his own hand, that strikes the fatal blow. In Deuteronomy 32:39–42 the Lord is depicted in a similar vengeful mode:

> See now that I myself am He!
>   There is no god besides me.
> I put to death and I bring to life,
>   I have wounded and I will heal,
>   and no one can deliver out of my hand.
> I lift my hand to heaven and declare:
>   As surely as I live for ever,
> when I sharpen my flashing sword
>   and my hand grasps it in judgement,
> I will take vengeance on my adversaries
>   and repay those who hate me.
> I will make my arrows drunk with blood,
>   while my sword devours flesh:
> the blood of the slain and the captives,
>   the heads of the enemy leaders.

If the avenging sword of the covenant reaches Israel's southernmost enemy, can Judah expect to escape?

To the north: Assyria (2:13–15)

The final nation to be identified as the object of God's displeasure is Assyria. This nation's power had been significantly weakened by the time of Josiah's ascendancy. Nevertheless, if she chose to do so, she still possessed sufficient resources to make short work of Judah. But ultimately all things are in the hands of the Lord Almighty, and he has determined against her.

1. Reduced to a wasteland

The voice once more is Zephaniah's and, in the name of the Lord, the prophet declares that:

> He will stretch out his hand against the north
> and destroy Assyria,
> leaving Nineveh utterly desolate
> and dry as the desert   (2:13).

Although the Lord's hand is stretched out against the whole nation, the city of Nineveh is particularly singled out as the object of almost unbelievable desolation. This formerly great and proud city shall be reduced to a desert-like wasteland. This prophecy was literally fulfilled following the fall of Nineveh in 612 BC to the new Babylonian world order. Nearly two centuries later the Greek historian Xenophon passed by the site on which Nineveh had once so proudly stood and could not find a trace of its existence.[6]

The utter destruction of this once-great city will be emphasized by the fact that:

> Flocks and herds will lie down there,
> creatures of every kind.
> The desert owl and the screech owl
> will roost on her columns.
> Their calls will echo through the windows,
> rubble will be in the doorways,
> the beams of cedar will be exposed   (2:14).

The picture is one of a city completely overrun by both domestic and wild animals. Flocks and herds are described as making their home among the ruins, as have the kind of birds that had once been identified as 'unclean' by God's law (Leviticus 11:13-19; Deuteronomy 14:11-18). The doors which would normally have been expected to keep most of these intruders out could no longer do so. The 'beams of cedar', signs of their former luxurious lifestyle (2 Samuel 7:2, 7; 1 Kings 5:6, 8; Jeremiah 22:14-16), are now completely disregarded. Chaos reigns!

2. An object of scorn and contempt

How different all this is to the city that once was! The prophet now highlights this contrast between the secure and complacent city that it had been and what it was destined to become. He begins: 'This is the carefree city that lived in safety' (2:15).

Palmer Robertson comments: 'A city rejoices when everyone prospers, when the economy is good, when the arts flourish, and the populace has time for leisure. No overburdening sense of responsibility and care oppresses the people.'[7] This is the pleasure that the Assyrians once enjoyed. There was a time when the surrounding nations were in awe of Assyria; she 'called the shots'. It seemed that there was nothing that this nation could not do. Indeed, there was nothing that she was not prepared to claim for herself. Her self-congratulation knew no bounds; self-existence was hers; the kind of language that ought to be reserved for the Lord alone was to be found on her lips: 'She said to herself, "I am, and there is none besides me"' (2:15; cf. Deuteronomy 4:39; Isaiah 45:5-6; 47:10). With such sentiments Assyria had sealed her own fate. She had placed herself in opposition to God. She had sought to appropriate to herself the kind of invincibility that none but God can claim. She was destined for a terrible fall. Speaking as though the prophecy had already been fulfilled, and summarizing what he has already declared, the prophet says, 'What a ruin she has become, a lair for wild beasts!' And, even worse than this, 'All who pass by her scoff and shake their fists.' No one is in awe of this great city any more. No one is afraid of her. Even those who merely pass by treat the memory of her boasts with scorn and contempt.

A warning to Judah

The first great lesson to be learned from all of this is that ungodliness and unrighteousness will be punished wherever they are found. None should imagine that they will be able to escape. This is true of Philistia, of Moab and Ammon, of Cush, and even the mighty Assyria. And if this is true of them, it will also be true of Judah. Indeed, the very reason for these announcements is to summon Judah to repentance. There is very little time before the Day of the Lord comes and it is imperative that the people should prepare themselves. Their only hope, as was previously announced (2:1–3), is that they humble themselves before God in genuine repentance. They must not try to convince themselves that this day will not come. Let what God has pronounced concerning the surrounding nations serve as a warning to them. It is still possible that a remnant may be saved to enjoy the plunder of their defeated enemies. But the big question remains, will Judah listen?

Points to ponder

Several important reminders are suggested by the portion of Scripture that we have just considered.

1. The God of the Bible is the God of the entire world.

Although history reveals that he has shown a special kindness to Israel, establishing ancient covenants with this people, God has never relinquished his sovereign rights over any part of the world that he has made. He is not the local deity of liberal theological mythology. He is the Creator and sustaining

Sovereign of the entire universe. There is not a place where his creatures can hide or escape his jurisdiction.

2. The God of the Bible is one who will oppose ungodliness and unrighteousness wherever they are to be found (Romans 1:18).
All people will be judged according to their works (Romans 2:6) and in a manner consistent with the light they have received (Romans 2:12). This will not leave any innocent, but it will mean that some are more guilty than others. Therefore, those who are outside the sphere of the gospel's influences will still be judged for what they have done and according to the light they have received (Romans 2:14–15). Those who enjoy the privilege of being within reach of special revelation, and all the blessings it offers, are in a worse danger. 'God does not show favouritism' (Romans 2:11). If we fall under God's judgement, we shall have no one to blame but ourselves.

3. The God of the Bible is so jealous over the welfare of his people that to oppose them is to place oneself in serious jeopardy.
It is to oppose God. Some of the nations in the portion of Scripture that we have been considering were particularly guilty of this folly. But to oppose the people of God is to oppose God himself, and there is no greater madness in the world. The church is, and always has been, 'the apple of his eye', the delight of his heart, the special object of his love. He has in fact loved them 'with an everlasting love' (Jeremiah 31:3; cf. Romans 8:28–39). It is a terrible folly to oppose those whom God has loved everlastingly.

4. Such is the compassion of the God of the Bible towards his people that he is capable of using even his judgements on some as warnings and inducements to repentance among others.
There is undoubted mystery here. It is beyond our full

comprehension. Nevertheless, this is what God did time and again for Israel. It is for us to heed the lessons of history and to make good use of them by seeking our God.

7

God's judgement will embrace Jerusalem

Please read Zephaniah 3:1-8

There is a saying which reminds us of the simple truth that 'There's none so blind as those who will not see.' This was certainly true of the inhabitants of Jerusalem in the sixth century before Christ. No matter who was sent to inform the people of their impending doom, they simply would not believe that such a thing could ever happen to them. After all, they were the specially chosen people of God: 'Theirs is the adoption as sons; theirs the divine glory, the covenants, the receiving of the law, the temple worship and the promises' (Romans 9:3-4).

Therefore, although God had sent them a faithful prophet in the person of Zephaniah, they could not accept, even from him, a message that identified them as the principal objects of the Lord's wrath. They were ready to believe that God could visit their neighbours in judgement. Indeed, they could rejoice in it. But they could not believe that this wrath was destined to fall on them as well. Therefore, having dealt with the surrounding nations, in the first eight verses of chapter 3 Zephaniah focuses almost exclusively once more on Jerusalem and on the judgement that will fall upon that city.

A surprising switch

Although the name of that ancient city is not specifically mentioned in this section, it quickly becomes apparent that Jerusalem is the true object of the prophet's crushing denunciations. She alone can be described as having such a relationship to 'the LORD' (3:5) that, in a special sense, he can be regarded as 'her God' (3:2). Furthermore, this same Lord would soon be described as being 'within her'—something that was only possible for those who could be considered as being in a special covenant relationship with him.

But the full force of what is recorded here, and the effect that it would have had upon the inhabitants of Jerusalem, can easily be overlooked. This is particularly so due to the chapter divisions in our Bibles (not to mention the well-intentioned sub-titles frequently added to some editions). This tends to disguise the impact that would have been felt by the original recipients of this part of the message. What we must keep in mind is the fact that anyone hearing the original declaration would automatically and initially have thought that they were still hearing a denunciation of one of the pagan cities—in this case, an announcement of judgement on Nineveh (2:13–15). Therefore, there would have been no initial sense of alarm. The complacent response of the inhabitants of Jerusalem would have been that of self-righteous glee. As far as they were concerned, this coming judgement was only what those wicked people deserved. It would not be until they reached the second verse of the third chapter that it would begin to dawn on them that the real focus of these stunning words was not some foreign city, but their own—Jerusalem and its inhabitants; the city of God.

So it is no longer the judgement soon to befall Assyria that is uppermost in the mind of Zephaniah—the spokesman of God—but the inhabitants of Jerusalem. Now, as a city of great wickedness (3:1–4), and one that has repeatedly despised God's overtures of mercy (3:5–7), she is to be brought along with others to judgement (3:8). In this section God is making it abundantly clear that this city and its inhabitants will not escape wrath. Its full and just measure will be meted out coincidentally with the arrival of 'the day' (3:8).

A city of great wickedness (3:1–4)

The words of this section begin with a lament: 'Woe to the city of oppressors, rebellious and defiled!' (3:1). The city's three most damning characteristics are—to follow the preferred order of the NKJV—rebellion, pollution and oppression. It is these characteristics that deservedly draw forth this 'woe'. It is a terrible indictment against this city. As the city chosen by God to be his special dwelling place, and the great centre of the nation with whom he had voluntarily entered into covenant, Jerusalem had become as faithless and corrupt as her neighbours. Indeed, because she had been favoured with greater privileges than they, her guilt was so much worse.

1. General characteristics

The first thing that the prophet does is to identify the general characteristics of this city's wickedness (3:1). She has shown herself to be 'rebellious'. Some of the specific ways in which this characteristic has manifested itself will become all too apparent in verse 2. But for the moment it is enough for us to observe that she has defiantly and obstinately refused the will of her Sovereign Lord. Some years later, when the prophet Jeremiah warned Jerusalem that the Babylonians—God's most immediate agents of doom—were on the march against the nation's cities, the main reason given by the Lord for this action was that 'she has rebelled against me' (Jeremiah 4:17).

The tragedy of her position is further compounded by the fact that she is 'defiled' (or 'polluted'), and therefore disqualified from any true service to God. That this should be true of the very people for whom a holy service was meant to be the purpose of her existence, and the essence of her relationship with God, is certainly a cause for lament. But this is not all. The nation that was wonderfully delivered from the oppression of Egypt, and was warned against adopting this stance towards others (cf. Exodus 22:21; Leviticus 19:13), has herself become the oppressor. She has become 'the city of oppressors'. As we shall see, plunder and fraud have become her hallmarks.

2. Specific manifestations

With the second verse, Zephaniah begins to put flesh on the bones of his earlier, more general, denunciation, and details the specific manifestations of this city's wickedness (3:2). Her rebellion is, of course, supremely directed against God. 'She obeys no one' (literally, 'She listens to no voice'). Her disobedience is connected with the voice of God and the variety of ways in which he has made his will known to the people. In particular they have refused to listen to his law, and to the prophets who have repeatedly been sent to them.

Not only have the inhabitants of Jerusalem failed to listen, but they have rejected every God-given attempt to restore them through discipline: 'she accepts no correction'. It is not as though God had spoken once, or twice, and then simply given up on them. He had extended his fatherly hand in chastisement throughout their long and often rebellious history (cf. Hebrews 12:5–6). Moreover, he had done so more recently during the time of the Assyrian dominance and through the reigns of Ahaz, Hezekiah and Manasseh, but still they would neither listen nor turn back to him in repentance. This complaint finds an echo in the later accusations brought against the people through the ministry of Jeremiah (see Jeremiah 2:30; 5:3; 7:27–29; 32:33; 35:13). Their response is simply to harden their hearts against the Lord. Moreover, 'She does not trust in the Lord.' It is not merely, or even primarily, that she has refused to respond to the Lord's *threats*; she has even been deaf to the *promises* that he has repeatedly brought before her. Ultimately, of course, every wicked way had really stemmed from this. Calvin says that unbelief is 'the mother of all the evil deeds by which men wilfully wrong and injure one another'.[1] We might also add that it is through unbelief that men and women most injure their Creator God.

The final indictment that is brought against this city is frequently associated with worship in the Old Testament: 'She does not draw near to her God.' The Hebrew word here actually means 'to approach God *properly* in worship'. In Judah's case this may well imply that although the people may still go through the external motions of offering some form of worship to God, they are incapable of, or are guilty of withholding, true worship's primary requirement: 'spirit and truth' (John 4:24). Under the Old Covenant too, the Lord's greatest complaint is that:

These people come near to me with their mouth
    and honour me with their lips,

> but their hearts are far from me.
> Their worship of me
>   is made up only of rules taught by men   (Isaiah 29:13).

As Palmer Robertson comments, 'Approaching the Almighty must always include adoration. Approach to God may be for the purpose of making petition, seeking counsel, offering a gift, or expressing praise. But in each case, the act of drawing near must involve worship and adoration. If he is God, every approach to him must be made worshipfully.'[2]

This all adds up to one thing: God has been rejected by his people. In return, he has rejected them.

3. Widespread scope

Having spoken of the general characteristics of this city's wickedness, and then extended these to specific areas, the prophet now moves on to the scope of this city's wickedness (3:3-4). If rebellion, pollution and oppression are characteristics of the city's population in general, then her civil and religious leaders are identified as bearing a particular responsibility for setting the overall tone. Oppression and pollution are very much in evidence here. Set aside for lofty responsibilities, government officials, on the one hand, and those considered prophets and priests, on the other, are guilty of behaving in the most contemptible manner. As is normal when such things happen, it is the ordinary and the most godly who suffer most. Those who should be able to look with confidence to their leaders for justice and example find themselves betrayed and exploited instead.

Zephaniah begins with *the oppression of the government officials* (3:3). Of them he says:

Her officials [princes (NKJV)] are roaring lions,
    her rulers [judges (NKJV)] are evening wolves
    who leave nothing for the morning.

The tragedy here is that those whose specific calling was
meant to secure protection for the weakest and stability for
society as a whole could be likened to ferocious wild animals,
intent on feeding on those whom they were supposed to govern.
Commenting on the final clause of this verse, David Baker
gruesomely reminds us that these animals 'do their work so
well that there are no bones left to "gnaw" [AV]'.3 A particularly
sad aspect of this entire tragedy is suggested by the reference
to the emptiness of the morning. This was the time normally
associated with legal judgement and justice (3:5; cf. 2 Samuel
15:2; Psalm 101:8; Jeremiah 21:12), but none exists. With leaders
like these, it is little wonder that the nation as a whole had gone
astray.

The prophet immediately couples the wickedness of the
nation's government officials with *the defilement of her religious
leaders* (3:4). These men are no better. First of all, 'Her prophets
are arrogant; they are treacherous men.' These charges may infer
that these men were simply guilty of speaking when God had
not spoken. This in itself would have been bad enough. Under
the law such action warranted the death penalty (Deuteronomy
18:20). But it might also mean that these prophets were
functioning without any specific calling from God (Micah 2:11;
3:5,11).

Commenting on these words, Baker writes, 'The *prophets*
are supposed to be the intermediaries between God and man,
accurately and unflinchingly presenting the divine will. Rather
than basing their words on the sure and faithful foundation of

God's revelation, they speak words of their own which have no more solid foundation than do the tossing sea waters (Genesis 49:4; cf. Judges 9:4; Jeremiah 23:32).'4

This fact invites the question: 'Why would anyone seek to do such a thing?'—to which there is an obvious answer. In those days an unscrupulous prophet could gain all sorts of advantages by being among those who had national influence. Therefore here were men who were not only arrogant before God, but whose sole purpose in assuming this particular role in the life of the nation was to gain some sort of temporal advantage for themselves, and almost certainly at the expense of ordinary people.

The nation's priests were just as culpable. Their chief responsibility was to represent men before God. This they did in connection with the administration of the sacrificial system and by teaching the law of God. But the charge against them is that they had done despite to both aspects of this responsibility: 'Her priests profane the sanctuary and do violence to the law.' For them there was no longer any meaningful distinction between the holy and the profane. Ultimately this was to lead to the abomination of allowing the nation's children to be offered as burnt sacrifices. Of all the profanities indulged by the people in their long and terrible history this ranks among the worst.

Not only was this a terrible profanity, it was expressly forbidden by the very law that these people were charged to uphold. Anticipating the terrible possibility that the nation might switch its allegiance from the one true and living God to the idols of the nations around them, God had specifically issued a command prohibiting the abomination to which they eventually succumbed. In Leviticus 18:21 we read, 'Do not give any of your children to be sacrificed to Molech, for you must not profane the name of your God. I am the LORD.' Again, immediately prior to Israel's entry into the promised land, and speaking of the ever-present temptation to justify idolatrous practices through some form of syncretistic worship, the Lord reminds his people: 'You must not worship the LORD your God *in their way*, because in worshipping their gods, they do all kinds of detestable things the LORD hates. They even burn their sons and daughters in the fire as sacrifices to their gods' (Deuteronomy 12:31, emphasis added; cf. 18:10). To their great shame, they had even indulged in this practice during the reigns of Ahaz (2 Kings 16:3) and Manasseh (2 Kings 21:6).

Even before they had finally stooped to this terrible practice, the priests had proved themselves unworthy of the trust that had been invested in them. Among their many responsibilities, priests were meant to act alongside judges in the administration of justice within the land (Deuteronomy 17:8–9). But part of the charge brought against them in Zephaniah's day was that they 'do violence to the law'. Not only did this cause havoc in the lives of those seeking justice, but it was also against the very law that they had been called upon to uphold! If those who disputed their decisions were worthy of death (Deuteronomy 17:10–12), what would the fate be of those who brutalized the law of God? (cf. Matthew 23:2, 13–36, 37–39).

A city that had repeatedly spurned mercy (3:5–7)
The next group of verses presents us with a stark contrast between the character and ways of the people of Judah, on the one hand, and those of the God of the covenant, on the other. Through them we are reminded of a series of remarkable truths about the Lord, truths that highlight the fact that God has always been ready to show mercy.

1. She has spurned his presence and justice

Firstly, evidence of God's mercy is seen in the reality of his abiding presence and dispensation of justice (3:5). The wonder is that he is still in their midst. In spite of all their wicked ways, 'the LORD' is still 'within her'. This is remarkable in and of itself. He who is 'of purer eyes than to behold evil, and [can] not look on iniquity' (Habakkuk 1:13, AV) is still among the people. It was, of course, of the essence of his ancient covenant promise to Israel that he would be present among his people (Exodus 29:42–46), and his faithfulness to that promise can be measured by the fact of his presence even now. Nevertheless, though he is still in her midst, he remains what he has always been: 'The LORD within her is righteous.' This confirmation finds further explanation in the words that immediately follow: 'he does no wrong' (cf. Deuteronomy 32:4). Not only is the contrast between him and them confirmed, but these words are an assertion of the plain fact that their wickedness has not changed him. His presence among them cannot be taken to imply a compromise on his part. He remains ever the same. As he reminded the people of Malachi's day, 'I am the LORD, I do not change' (Malachi 3:6, NKJV). He may change his acts but, as Calvin so quaintly puts it, '... he changes not his nature to suit the humour of men.'[5]

What he is, of course, is righteous—and what a righteous God does is to dispense justice: 'Morning by morning he dispenses his justice, and every new day he does not fail.' This statement may simply refer to the reality of a testimony to his presence due to the ongoing existence of the sacrificial system; the daily sacrifices were still being offered. But it may also refer to the existence of a remnant of faithful judges still sitting at the gate of the city dispensing justice. What it most certainly indicates is that all has not yet failed in this once-great city. The fact that God is present, and with every new dawn is found still dispensing justice, is at least an indication that the influences of his common grace have not been entirely withdrawn. In the midst of overwhelming wickedness, he has been continually and dependably present among this people. This reveals something of the commitment that exists on his part to their well-being.

However, in the long term, this offers no comfort for the people. They had made it their boast that God was ever present with them. But the promise of God's presence is a two-edged sword. While his presence can signify salvation—as indeed it does later in the chapter (cf. 3:17)—here the same presence threatens judgement (cf. Hosea 11:9). Therefore it was madness for the people to flatter themselves with the thought that God would continually bear with their wickedness. But flatter themselves they did, as is clear from the final painful clause of this verse: '... yet the unrighteous know no shame.' This is their response to his presence, his kindness and his mercy. The contrast between their wickedness and his righteousness should inspire repentance, but it does not. By now they have so hardened themselves as to be incapable of even acknowledging any wrongdoing. As the seventeenth-century Puritan, George Hutcheson, remarks, 'They were as earnest to go wrong as he was to reclaim them.'[6]

2. She has spurned his warning examples

Secondly, evidence of God's mercy is seen in the way he has dealt with the surrounding nations (3:6). As we have already seen, the story of what God had done to these nations provides ample evidence of the kind of fate that awaits those who persist in wickedness and ignore his commands. Judah can expect the same if she persists in wickedness and ignores his warnings. What had God done to the surrounding nations? The answer is found in verse 6. With the personal pronoun coming back into play, God speaks of what he has done to them: 'I have cut off nations; their strongholds are demolished.' So thorough had been his judgement against them that they are spoken of as if they no longer exist. Their 'strongholds' could be a reference to the corner towers of the city. It is certainly a reference to the most strongly fortified points of their city walls. But what had become of them? They were 'demolished'; they lie in ruins. Moreover:

> I have left their streets deserted,
>   with no one passing through.
> Their cities are destroyed;
>   no one will be left—no one at all.

What a graphic picture this is! Streets that were once teeming with activity are now empty. Like the eeriness often associated with so-called 'ghost towns', their very emptiness is suggestive of the terrible calamity that had overtaken them. Once-proud cities have been reduced to rubble and stand as monuments to the folly of arrogance and corruption. And it is 'cities' (plural) that have been afflicted in this way—not just one, but many. God has repeatedly shown that he is a God who judges wickedness, wherever it is found. Will Judah not learn from such experiences? Will she stubbornly and foolishly go on ignoring the lessons of history? Will she not be startled out of her complacency and turn from her wickedness?

But this raises another question: why has God done this to the surrounding nations? God's motive in judging them is twofold: first, in relation to the nations themselves, his judgement of them is the result of their own wickedness. God's judgement is always just. They are judged for their own sins. If it should be asked why it is that the axe should fall precisely when it does, it can only be assumed that the time of 'fulness' has been reached (cf. Genesis 15:16; Deuteronomy 20:17; Judges 11:23). We need ever to remember that sin forfeits 'rights' before God. For sinners to seek justice from God is a most precarious enterprise. What we need is mercy! Justice always threatens our existence. The surprising thing is that we are allowed to go on in our sinfulness, that we are not brought to hell immediately. There is mystery in this, but of one thing we can be sure: God has his purposes, and faith must learn to trust him to do what is right, and at just the right time.

And this is where the second discernible motive comes in. He specifically tells us here that a major consideration in the judgement of the surrounding nations is that the judgement itself should act as an example and warning to his own people and city. This aspect of God's character is not rare in the Bible. Time after time he makes known that he is willing to delay and withhold punishment in order that the people might learn and turn from their sinful ways (see Exodus 34:6–7; Numbers 14:18–19; Amos 4:6–11; 7:1–6; Romans 9:22–24). This is clearly a major consideration in his dealings with these people even now. He says:

> I said to the city,
>> 'Surely you will fear me
>> and accept correction!'

To which a promise is immediately added: 'Then her dwelling would not be cut off, nor all my punishments come upon her' (3:7). In other words, if the right response were forthcoming, even now people would not be lost. They could still avoid the fate of the nations.

As Calvin says, 'Here God assumes the character of man, as he does often elsewhere: for he does not wait for what is future, as though he was doubtful; but all things, as we know, are before his eyes.'7 He does this in order to show how inexcusable the nation really is. Although much has been said in this book about God's determination to judge sinfulness, it should never be suggested that there is anything other than a genuine longing within God to be merciful. This has been the consistent witness of history from the time sin entered the world through Adam, on through the age of the patriarchs and through to the establishment of the nation of Israel. And although sin has often been rampant among this privileged people, as it was at this very moment, God still longs to awaken within them concerns about their wickedness and a longing to return to him.

Sadly, this was not to be: 'But they were still eager to act corruptly in all they did' (3:7). This shows how deep and inexcusable was their opposition to God and his ways. They would not be instructed, not even by the calamities that had fallen on the nations around them. Indeed, they seemed to go from bad to worse. Nothing of this had, of course, taken God by surprise. He knows what is in the heart of man; that 'every inclination of the thoughts of his heart was only evil all the time' (Genesis 6:5). Indeed, there are clear echoes of the days of the Flood here. Moses too had declared that after his death the nation would become 'utterly corrupt' (Deuteronomy 31:29). Therefore, judgement was inevitable.

An announcement of universal judgement (3:8)

And so, once more, a terrible announcement of judgement is made. God's long patience has seemingly accomplished nothing. The people have simply become worse. So now he announces his intention to come and, when he comes, it will be with a drawn sword. There are several things that ought to be noticed about the particular form of this announcement.

1. It is certain to come

The first thing that the Lord does is to call upon the people to *wait* for this coming judgement. '"Therefore wait for me," declares the LORD.' But there is a telling note of certainty that shines through this declaration. The emphasis is on the fact that he will most definitely come. George Hutcheson finds a particular encouragement in this statement for the true people of God. He suggests that the very certainty of the Lord's coming should act as an incentive to the godly remnant to live patiently in the midst of adversity. After all, when 'that day' arrives, he will right all wrongs.[8] This conviction is undoubtedly true, but it seems more likely that the main emphasis here is simply on the certainty that this event itself will take place.

2. God will be an active participant

The narrative then goes on to make abundantly clear that the Lord will be an active participant in the judgement that is to come. This is not just a matter of God exercising his judgement through secondary agents. He is in the forefront of the action. This is confirmed no matter how the next clause is translated. The completed sentence reads: '"Therefore wait for me," declares the LORD, "for the day I will stand up to testify."' The translation of the NIV follows that of the Septuagint and the Syriac version. If this rendering is to be preferred then the Lord is not merely bringing the people to trial, but he is himself the chief prosecution witness.

The NKJV follows the Hebrew alternative, relegated to a footnote in the NIV: 'Therefore wait for me, says the LORD, *until the day I rise up for plunder.*' In this case the theme of the mighty

Warrior is carried through as God is seen gaining his just deserts in the judgement of the people.

No matter how this clause is translated, there can be no doubt that the Lord is immediately and actively involved in the judgement. Indeed, the rest of this verse presents us with the picture of an angry God pouring out his wrath on the people.

3. It will engulf all nations
Finally, when this day of judgement comes, it will engulf all the nations of the world. First, the Lord says:

I have decided to assemble the nations,
   to gather the kingdoms,
and to pour out my wrath on them—
   all my fierce anger   (3:8).

These sentiments, and especially those that immediately follow, again remind us of the great flood during the days of Noah. That day too was a 'Day of the Lord'. This time we are informed that 'The whole world will be consumed by the fire of my jealous anger.' Jerusalem will be included in this day of destruction, but so too will all the world's nations. A universal calamity is envisaged. When Jesus Christ was found preaching the terrors of God's coming judgement, his message combined the destruction of Jerusalem with the end of the world in such a way that they could hardly be separated (Matthew 24). So intimately connected are the events surrounding the destruction of Jerusalem in AD 70 with that great Day which shall bring a final end to all God's judgements that the one can be seen as a foreshadowing of the other. Likewise, the prophecy brought through the mouth of Zephaniah can both anticipate the Fall of Jerusalem in 586 BC and provide a picture of the judgement to come at the end of the world. In that final judgement, devastation falls upon all the nations of the world.

God tells the people to 'wait'. This does not mean that the wait will be long and tedious. It means that the people of God must wait, trusting that the day will certainly arrive. They must not entertain doubts. They must live in ways that provide a living witness to their hope in God, and this testimony is to be maintained in the midst of a persistent refusal to fear the Lord even among those who profess his name.

Points to ponder
The reason given in this section for the judgement of Jerusalem is the wickedness of its inhabitants. As we come to the end of this part of Zephaniah's prophecy, and prepare to turn to happier things, we ought just to pause and take a final look at the concept of wickedness that is presented to us here. The two most common words used in the Old Testament are usually translated by the words 'ungodly' (or, 'wicked') and 'evil'. Given the context of Zephaniah 3:1–8, it seems appropriate to pursue three lines of thought in connection with this word.

1. It reminds us that wickedness is first and foremost against God.
It is 'ungodliness'. King David saw this quite clearly. Having committed adultery with another man's wife, and having sent her husband to his death, he was eventually confronted with an accusing finger. Nathan the prophet had boldly stood before his earthly sovereign and exposed his duplicity with the stunning declaration: 'You are the man!' (2 Samuel 12:7). David's response was one of brokenness. He knew that he had behaved wickedly. But he also knew that, no matter how much he had wronged others, it was against God that he had sinned most of all. In

Psalm 51:4 he acknowledges before God that 'Against you, you only, have I sinned and done what is evil in your sight.'

Commenting on this statement, James Montgomery Boice writes, 'First, sin by its very definition is against God, since it is only by God's law that sin is defined as sin. A wrong done to our neighbour is an offence against humanity. In the eyes of the state, which measures wrongs by its own laws, that wrong may be a crime. Only before God is it a sin. Second, it is only because God is in the picture that even a wrong done to our neighbour is a wrong. It is because our neighbour is made in God's image and is endowed with rights by God that it is wrong to harm him or her.'[9] Incidentally, this is also why all sin must be punished; it is against God.

2. It reminds us that there is something very contagious about wickedness.
If sin is not corrected, its influence is likely to spread. Indeed, so destructively powerful is it that, but for God's restraining influence, men would become devils and earth would become hell. It is true that one of the mercies of 'common grace' is that God does restrain the effects of sin in the world. Nevertheless, no one should underestimate the potentially serious and damaging consequences of a sinful example. This is so whether the sphere of authority for which we have responsibility is the home, the church, the workplace, or the nation. If wickedness is allowed to flourish unhindered in any of these spheres, the long-term potential for harm is enormous. Moreover, the worst thing that can happen to us is that God should give us over to our wickedness; that he should just allow us to do what we want (Romans 1:24–31). The Christian takes enormous comfort from the fact that the Lord disciplines those whom he loves (Hebrews 12:4–11).

3. It reminds us that wickedness will not triumph.

The promise of Scripture is that, no matter how rampant the advance of wickedness may become, it will not be victorious. All the wicked, both men and angels, will be brought before God's great Day of Judgement (2 Corinthians 5:10; Hebrews 9:27; Jude 6; Revelation 20:7–15). This fact also implies that, no matter what the appearances might be, wickedness is never finally out of control (see Job 1–2).

Part 3:

His coming for restoration (3:9–20)

God will restore hope to all his people

Please read Zephaniah 3:9–13

Thus far the prophet has concentrated on the primary aspect of his message: it is one of wrath and anger. 'The day of the LORD's wrath' is coming and 'the whole world will be consumed' in his jealous anger (1:18; cf. 2:2–3; 3:8). Although there have been hints of mercy along the way (2:1–3), the overwhelming emphasis has been to couple the Lord's coming with the wrath that will be revealed at that time.

Given the kind of God that the Lord is, and the kind of people who now inhabit his world, this emphasis is somewhat inevitable. He is holy and just; we are sinners. When these realities are brought into close proximity to each other, the outcome is never in doubt. Sin must be punished. For God not to pour out his wrath would mean the end of God! Evil, in all its ugliness and confusion, would then prevail—and this could never be. He is the Sovereign Lord, and he must and will prevail.

But this also means that sin must finally be punished (3:8) and, when it is, that most terrible day described in this prophecy will have arrived (1:14–18).

Another side to 'that day'—restoration

But there is to be another side to this same day. That we are still thinking about the same day is suggested by the simple use of the opening word in verse 9: 'Then …' The use of this word is intended to show that the same day that will bring distress and darkness to many will also bring blessing and encouragement to others. The very day that brings judgement will also be a day of restoration. This is confirmed by the use of the now familiar words, 'On that day …', with which verse 11 also opens. This other side to that day is now the main focus for the rest of this prophetic book (3:9–20).

1. It is a day of hope

On that day God will not only be seen as a holy judge, but as a loving parent. Moreover, the pain through which his people pass (and they will pass through it) will be to them a purifying agent. In other words, the pain will not be an end in itself, but the means to an end. It will be the means to the remnant's restoration. It is this promise of restoration that will provide the hope that the people will need if they are to get through the difficult days that lie ahead.

Hope is one of mankind's most fundamental needs; we are almost incapable of living without it. This is one of the reasons why a person will profess to 'live in hope' even when there are no rational grounds for doing so. By contrast, the kind of hope that the Bible is keen to commend is so different that all other hope is scarcely recognizable as hope at all.

Biblical hope, as R. V. G. Tasker says, 'is not a matter of temperament, nor is it conditioned by prevailing circumstances or any human possibilities. It does not depend upon what a man possesses, upon what he may be able to do for himself, nor upon what any other human being may do for him.'[1]

On the contrary, it is a hope which rests in a God 'who acts and intervenes in human life, and who can be trusted to implement His promises'.[2] These are the vital ingredients for any sure and certain hope, and they are found here.

2. It is the Lord's doing

The one who initiates the restoration, and therefore the hope, is the very one who also brings in the judgement. It is none other than the Warrior-King who is now portrayed as the one who graciously initiates the blessings to be experienced by his people. This is made clear by the 'I wills' that fill the entire landscape of the concluding section of this chapter: it is the Lord who purifies (3:9), who removes the proud and establishes the meek (3:11–12), and who preserves his people from their enemies (3:15). It is this same Lord who is with his people (3:15, 17), comforting them (3:18–19), and who will finally restore a complete state of well-being to them (3:20). Everything bestowed upon these people is due to the wonderful and all-encompassing grace of God. Through the eyes of these verses it is now possible to see that where once 'sin increased', grace is marvellously destined to 'increase all the more' (Romans 5:20).

3. It is for his people's benefit

But who will benefit from this restoration? Who are entitled to hope that this restoration to righteousness will be theirs? Two distinct groups emerge from the narrative. They are the Lord's 'scattered people' from the nations of the world (3:10), and 'the remnant of Israel' (3:13). As we give separate consideration to the blessings received by these two groups, we must keep in mind that they are both part of the one people of God. Eventually, that which they are already in essence will be true in obvious reality. Part of the blessing of that day is that they will then be seen to be united as one. But in order to experience the blessing held out to them, both will need to undergo the purification process that is necessary for this to be achieved.

Hope for the nations (3:9–10)

Given the opening words of this final section—'Then I will purify the lips of *the peoples*' and 'that *all of them* may call on the name of the Lord'—it might seem tempting to suggest that everybody will be restored. But this would be a grave mistake. There is no universalism in prospect here. The scope of the Lord's love and mercy is clearly specified: it is for the 'worshippers' and the 'scattered'; it is for 'the remnant' (3:13; cf. 2:7, 9). Nevertheless, there was yet another surprise in store for those originally on the receiving end of this prophecy.

Historically, when the people of Israel were spiritually at their best, they knew that the Lord had always preserved a remnant *among them.* But the surprising thing here is that the prophet anticipates a remnant that reaches beyond Israel's own ethnic and geographical borders. The 'all', the 'scattered', the 'worshippers' would also include those 'from beyond the borders of Cush'. Indeed, a hint of this spectacular largesse was given earlier, when the prophet announced that 'The nations on every shore will worship him' (2:11). Not only was this blessing to be conferred, but it would be done consistently with all that would be required to make it possible. This meant that they would be purified.

1. Their lips will be purified for worship

Indeed, one of the most notable distinctions between the generality of Jerusalem's 'defiled' inhabitants (3:1) and those truly blessed of the Lord is that he promises to purify the latter. The opening clause of this section reads, 'Then will I purify the lips of the peoples.' The aspect of this which is particularly singled out for mention is the purification of the lips. The New Testament reminds us that it is 'out of the overflow of the heart' that 'the mouth speaks' (Matthew 12:34) and therefore it is the lips that will provide the first expression of a transformation of heart. On 'that day', however, this evidence of transformation will not only be seen among the inhabitants of Jerusalem, nor will it be restricted to that class of people most clearly in need of it (3:3–4), but among all the scattered peoples of the world (3:10). No longer will the name of any false deity be on the lips of these people (cf. Hosea. 2:17). A truly glorious triumph of grace is envisaged.

Two purposes for this action are immediately given. The first is, 'that all of them may call on the name of the Lord'. This is clearly God's main purpose in graciously purifying the people— that they may be able to address him appropriately, that they may be able to offer him the worship that is his due. More will be said about this later. Quite understandably, however, a number of commentators have also recognized here an undoing of the curse of Babel (cf. Genesis 11:1–9). On that earlier occasion, the confusion of languages among the people was God's response to man's vain attempt to assert independence from him. But now new lips have been given so that he might, in unison with others, worship his Creator and Redeemer. The same connection between 'the day of the Lord' and the widespread '[calling] on the name of the Lord' is made first by the prophet

Joel (Joel 2:28–32), and then by the apostle Peter on the Day of
Pentecost (Acts 2:21).

2. Their hearts will be united in service

The second great expression of the transformation that will
take place in their hearts is that the people will be united in the
service of God. The third clause of verse 9 begins with 'and',
which is meant to emphasize the new oneness that exists among
these people, but it continues with the affirmation that they will
'serve him shoulder to shoulder' (3:9). This is a most impressive
picture. Those once divided by race and religion are now seen
to be side by side, determined to work together with a new
gladness in the service of the one true and living God. In his
Commentary on the Minor Prophets, Homer Hailey expresses it
like this: 'Yoked together in the Lord they strive together in one
great objective of service'.[3] Clearly, the new heart has led to 'the
dividing wall of hostility' being broken down (Ephesians 2:14).
The enmity that once existed between these peoples of different
nations has been demolished.

This same theme of former enemies finding common cause
is again taken up in verse 10, although this time worship is the
main theme. 'From beyond the rivers of Cush' would naturally
indicate a place beyond Ethiopia; 'the rivers', of course, refer
to 'the Nile and tributaries that flowed into it'.[4] But in order to
understand the full significance of this description it must be
remembered that, in the eighth century BC, Ethiopia itself would
have been regarded as an extremely remote region. Indeed,
according to Theo Laetsch, at that time anything to the south
of Ethiopia was regarded as 'the end of the world'.[5] The point
of this is that deep in the heart of Africa, and even beyond, 'my
worshippers, my scattered people will bring me offerings' (3:10;
cf. Psalm 72:10). There is sometimes a tendency to forget that

this had been anticipated in the annals of Israel's history (1 Kings 8:41–43; Psalm 22:27; 102:22; Isaiah 2:2–4; 18:7; 19:18–25; 45:14; 56:1–7; cf. Malachi 1:11; Acts 8:26–39). The offerings brought further emphasize the new-found unity of purpose that exists among the once-divided peoples.

3. An anticipation of distant events
Of course, all of this anticipates a fulfilment beyond the immediate historical circumstances of this particular prophet's message. It takes us on to the New Testament era and to those whom the apostle Paul refers to as having been 'grafted in' (Romans 11:17). It is through the proclamation of the gospel that this new age will be introduced and, with it, those blessings that will also eventually encompass 'a new heaven and a new earth, the home of righteousness' (2 Peter 3:13).

Nevertheless, even in the present context it is important to remember that the entire world is, as it has always been, the object of the Lord's care and concern. Although the nation of Israel had been greatly favoured, the entire creation and its population have always been on his mind (cf. Psalm 24:1; Genesis 12:3; Isaiah 19:23–25; Zechariah 8:23; Revelation 7:9). All the promises that focus on Jew *and Gentile* are fulfilled in Jesus Christ. It is through his sacrificial death on the cross that the artificial barriers between nations are finally broken down and the foundation of a new building—the church, made up of Jew and Gentile—is established (Ephesians 2:11–22). All this is so wonderfully anticipated here.

Hope for Jerusalem (3:11–13)
The inclusion of other nations does not mean that God has given up on his ancient chosen people. Indeed, initially at least, the blessings that will come to the Gentiles will come through

Israel. But even then not every individual within Israel will participate in the blessings promised here. Sadly, and with the benefit of hindsight, it is possible to see that most of the Jews would go on rejecting the Messiah.

Nevertheless, even from a nation that had so vilely abused its privileges and spurned its Lord's entreaties, some would seek God and be saved. Even though many were destined to fall under the Babylonian sword, a 'remnant of Israel' would be saved and from them a new day and people would emerge. Once again, it is the sovereign grace of God that is very much to the fore. On that day a great transformation will take place.

1. The cause of her shame will be purged

Earlier the rebellious inhabitants of Jerusalem had been described as shameless (3:5). But this is set to change. 'On that day', the Lord himself assures them, 'you will not be put to shame for all the wrongs you have done to me' (3:11). This statement is most telling. It is one thing for the shameless to profess no sense of shame; it is another to have the living God declare that no other person will be able to put them to shame.

This is not due to any false assessment having been previously made about the state of the lives of these people. They had undoubtedly sinned (3:5; 2:1). On the contrary, it is entirely due to God's gracious intervention that there will be no shame: 'because I will remove from this city those who rejoice in their pride'. Those who through their pride and arrogance had brought shame to the holy city will be removed. He is also determined that what will be done on that day will be of lasting significance. So thorough will be the purging of the remnant's guilt that 'Never again will you be haughty on my holy hill.' Once again, not only are we informed of what God will do, but we are given an insight into what he is like. Pride is an abomination to him. It is incompatible with his own character and will not be tolerated wherever he is present. It was this nation's pride that had brought her to the brink of destruction. Therefore, in order for there to be hope for Jerusalem, all her impure elements must be removed.

2. Those who exemplify grace will be preserved

Pride and haughtiness—'the arrogance of self-determination without God'[6]—are to be eradicated. In their place will be a people characterized by meekness, humility and faith: 'But I will leave within you the meek and humble' (3:12). These allusions to meekness and humility are not, as some commentators suppose, references to social status. Rather, as Palmer Robertson suggests, these are descriptions of moral attributes.[7] Here are a people who now see themselves as God sees them. They recognize that they have no merit before God. They are only fit to be consumed by the fire of God's anger (2:2). But having realized the true nature of their condition, with meekness and humility they have sought the refuge that was held out to them; they have sincerely sought the Lord and found his shelter (2:3).

To meekness and humility is added faith. What a difference a little humility makes! Earlier in this chapter, the self-reliant inhabitants of this city were characterized by rebellious unbelief (3:2). Now they are known as those 'who trust in the name of the LORD'. What a contrast this is! No longer is their hope in themselves; nor in any supposed power, wisdom, or riches to be found in this world. Instead, it is the Lord himself, and all that is represented by his name, who is the object of their trust. He is the self-existent, eternal and covenant-keeping God; his very name suggests that all that these people will ever need, in life or in death, is safely secured and provided by him.

3. Righteousness will be established in her midst

Righteousness now comes into view (3:13). Firstly, the lives of the people will conform to their new status: 'The remnant of Israel will do no wrong.' In verse 5 of this chapter it was said that 'The LORD ... does no wrong.' Now a day is anticipated when his people will be like him. They have truly been made anew. This is surely to be expected in those who have been re-created in the image of God. As Jonathan Edwards is keen to remind us in *The Religious Affections*, Christian practice is the chief evidence both to others and ourselves that a work of regeneration has taken place in the heart.[8] New patterns of behaviour begin to spring from a heart that has been made new. Of course, complete sanctification awaits a still further day, but the promise and down-payment are in place in those who have been saved by God's grace.

Secondly, the mouths of the people will reflect the state of their hearts. We are informed that '... they will speak no lies ...' This is in sharp contrast to the lies that had filled the mouths of their false prophets—lies that encouraged the people into idolatry (3:4; cf. 1:4–6). Like the Gentile nations, their lips have been purified too. But the promise goes even further than this: '... nor will deceit be found in their mouths.' The use of the word 'deceit' reminds us of Jacob who, certainly in his younger days, lived up to the figurative meaning of his name (i.e., 'he deceives'). Without doubt he deceived his father Isaac into giving him the blessing which was customarily reserved for the first-born (Genesis 27:35–36). His name was subsequently changed to 'Israel' (Genesis 35:10), and the nation would come to be named after him. Included in the promise is the assurance that all traces of deceit will be removed from Jacob's descendants.

4. The cause of her fear will be removed

Finally, the condition of the people will conform to their new status: 'They will eat and lie down ...' The scene has switched once more—this time from an urban city to a pastoral landscape. The people are now depicted as sheep in need of sustenance and protection. This is the special lot of those who have come to put their trust in the Lord, for those who have discovered that the Lord is their Shepherd. The relationship that they now enjoy is one of intimacy, one that assures of an abundance of provision.

To complete the bliss of this picture, perfect security is guaranteed: '... and no one will make them afraid.' How can this be? What has become of their enemies? The Warrior-King has made short work of them. Remember, the day that was destined to bring peace to his own people was also ordained to bring defeat and shame to his, and their, enemies.

Although both Jeremiah and Ezekiel employ the same phrase in connection with Israel's return from Babylonian exile (Jeremiah 30:10; 46:27; Ezekiel 34:28; 39:26), here is something beyond anything experienced on earth. Indeed, ultimately it sees beyond even the blessings of the new covenant era (although it includes the latter), to a new heaven and a new earth. David Baker concludes: 'When the Creator is worshipped and served as he ought to be, paradise is regained.'9 In grateful anticipation of such a day the people of God, whether Jew or Gentile, could join their hearts together in an experiential singing of the metrical version of the twenty-third psalm:

The Lord's my Shepherd, I'll not want;
He makes me down to lie,
In pastures green, he leadeth me,
The quiet waters by.

My soul he doth restore again,
And me to walk doth make;
Within the paths of righteousness
E'en for his own name's sake.

Yea, though I walk through death's dark vale,
Yet will I fear none ill;
For thou art with me and thy rod
And staff me comfort still.

My table thou has furnished
In presence of my foes;
My head thou dost with oil anoint
And my cup overflows.

Goodness and mercy all my life
Shall surely follow me;
And in God's house, for evermore,
My dwelling place shall be.

Points to ponder

R. V. G. Tasker says of Christian hope that it 'is not a kite at the mercy of the changing winds', but 'an anchor of the soul, both sure and steadfast, penetrating deep into the invisible eternal world (Hebrews 6:19)'.[10] This is the only kind of hope worth having.

1. In order to enjoy this kind of hope we must look for it in the right place.
Biblical Christianity only offers one hope for the entire world. If men and women wish to find acceptance before God on the Day of Judgement, then they must seek it in the way that he has provided for it. This is true no matter where we were born,

or in what religion we were brought up. There is an exclusivity about biblical religion; it will allow no rivals (Exodus 20:3-4; Isaiah 43:11; John 14:6; Acts 4:12). Modern pluralism proceeds on the assumption that religion is simply about man's search for God. Therefore, it is hardly surprising that sincerity in religion is considered the only thing that really matters. Although important, sincerity can never be enough for the God of truth, for the one who has clearly made himself known to man.

2. In order to enjoy this kind of hope we must seek it in the appointed way.

This means accepting that we have no hope except in God, and in his gracious provision for sin and sinners in Jesus Christ. Pride is the great evil here and must be dealt a fatal blow. We must ever remind ourselves of the fact that there is a standard of righteousness that is expected by God that we can never produce. Our past is simply against us: not only were we born 'dead in trespasses and sins', but with every moment of every day we have added our own iniquities. Even at our best we have fallen short of the standard that God has set for us (Matthew 22:34-40). Moreover, a mere glance at our past and present provides us with little in the way of optimism for the future. So thoroughly ingrained is our propensity to sin and self that even if the slate were suddenly wiped clean, we would never be able to keep it in this pristine condition. Thank God that in Jesus Christ there is a complete provision for all our needs. He has lived the kind of life we have never been able to live; he has died the death that we dare not die. Through his life and death he has become the grounds upon which God can justify the ungodly and provide for us the righteousness he requires. We, in meekness and humility, must cast ourselves upon him and his saving merits alone that we might find peace with God.

3. In order to enjoy this kind of hope we must expect it to produce a changed life.

Christian faith is not only a matter of knowing the truth and confessing it to be true. When a man or woman is genuinely brought to faith in Jesus Christ this is the result of a regenerating work of the Holy Spirit in the heart. This is how the mind is changed in the direction of truth; this is how the affections embrace the truth. But it is equally true that the chief way in which we and others detect this change is in our lives. God's concern in bringing us to faith in Jesus Christ is that we might be holy, that we might be increasingly like Jesus Christ in the moment-by-moment of our daily lives. This is something that will be seen in specific acts of devotion (the offering of ourselves in worship and service), the way we conduct ourselves in the ordinary events of life (with meekness, humility and trust), and particularly in the way we use our tongues. Although a properly balanced outlook must be maintained between what we are and what we shall soon be, we ought not to entertain hopes of heaven when there is little evidence of a changed life.

9

God will restore rejoicing among his people

Please read Zephaniah 3:14–17

How wonderful it is to emerge from the intense darkness and gloom of the greater part of this prophecy into the delights of this new environment of light and joy! It is true that the earlier picture is still very much part of the background to this new situation; indeed, in verse 16 we are again reminded that 'that day' is still part of this one. But there is an important difference: we are now on the other side of that day. We are breathing a new atmosphere; we are bathing in a new light. The dark clouds have been rolled away, and the sun has started to spread its warmth over us. The day may be the same, but somehow it is different.

One of the reasons that this new perspective is so different is that something has happened to the recipients of God's grace. They have, of course, been changed. Purity has replaced defilement; harmony has supplanted oppression, and submission has overcome rebellion (cf. 3:1, 9, 11–13). The 'Day of the Lord' has come, but it holds no fear for the people of God. They are at one with him now, and this is a great cause for celebration; it is a time for rejoicing. And this rejoicing is the great theme that is now placed on the lips of the prophet. He is himself overwhelmed with what has happened, and he expects these people to be so as well.

A call to rejoice (3:14)

The opening verse of this section contains an unrestrained summons to rejoice. As Palmer Robertson says, 'By piling up every available expression for joy, the prophet leaps across the vale of gloom into the realm of grace-beyond-devastation.'[1] Once again we are brought face-to-face with one of those surprising statements within Zephaniah's prophecy. After all that has been said about judgement, it might well have been thought that sadness and depression were a far more appropriate response to the announcements that have been made. But, as we saw in the last section (3:9–13), the prophet is looking beyond all this and urging God's chosen people to do the same.

1. There is to be a triumphant song

Owing to the reality of the existence of 'another side' to the judgement story, the first thing that the people of God are called upon to do is to sing in triumphant song. Indeed, they are to 'Sing … shout aloud … be glad and rejoice.' The term that is used for 'shout' is one that is often used in Scripture in connection with the cry given at the beginning of a battle (cf. Numbers 10:9; Joshua 6:10; 1 Samuel 17:20; 2 Chronicles 13:12, 15), the outcome of which is not believed to be in doubt. Coupled as it is with gladness and rejoicing, it is also reasonable to assume that these people are being called upon to rouse their faith and, as we shall go on to see, they have every good reason for doing so. Moreover, the kind of rejoicing that is expected is not half-hearted. Each person is told to rejoice 'with all your heart'. They are to shake off all sense of reserve and doubt. They are to rejoice as though the victory had already been won, even though its reality is still some way off.

2. The people of God are to sing this song

And who is it that is to rejoice in this way? It is the people of God: 'O daughter of Zion ... O Israel ... O daughter of Jerusalem!' The very mention of these names—two geographical (Zion, Jerusalem) and one ethnic (Israel)—would have brought back wonderful memories of God's gracious dealings with his people in the past. But it is not just, or even primarily, the past that is in this prophet's mind now. He is concerned with both the present and a most glorious future that is in store for these people. He refers to the city as 'daughter'—the simple explanation being that the Hebrew word for 'city' is feminine. This daughter is, however, the reassembled remnant of Israel. As such she has a special relationship with her Lord and therefore she is entitled to the confidence that goes with such a relationship.

The victory that these people are being called upon to anticipate is clearly beyond their natural capacity to attain. But, as with all the blessings of God, the people themselves are not being called upon to attain it. The Lord will gain the victory for them. They are simply called upon to trust the one who will bring it to pass. Calvin says that the purpose is 'that in their exile and extreme distress they might yet prepare themselves to give thanks to God, as though they were already, as they say, in possession of what they had prayed for'.[2] The reason is beyond dispute: that which is in the mind of God is as good, or as sure, as something that is already accomplished.

This act of rejoicing is not only a great statement of faith in the Word of God, but it might also have the knock-on effect of helping these people face up to the demands of their present struggles. No doubt many of us have had some experience of how this kind of thing might work at the psychological level—what some have referred to as 'the power of sympathy'.[3] For example, a large crowd assembles at a sports stadium determined to rouse its favourite team to victory. A small section of the crowd begins to sing and chant and shout for the side they wish to win. The noise is contagious. Before long others have joined in and the sound of their singing echoes around the stadium. The crowd's enthusiasm is soon communicating itself to those on the field of play. They are now moving forward with a new energy and purpose. Even though they started the game as underdogs, there is a new sense of belief among them now; they really think they can go on to victory.

There is, of course, one serious snag to our illustration. No matter how strong the support for the players may be, and no matter how much the players may be buoyed up by it, the team may simply not be up to the task in front of them. Despite all the best efforts of the crowd, all comes to nothing. Everyone returns to his or her home disappointed. But not so in the case before us. When the people of God put their trust in the Word of God, they are not pinning their hopes on 'the power of sympathy'. The great shout that goes up from their mouths is not merely an expression of their own hopes. Faith is anchored to something much more reliable. It rests on a substantial body of information that is provided by God himself, in the revelation that he has given in his infallible Word. Therefore, when these people sing and shout and rejoice, it is because they know something of who God is, what he is like and what he can do. Their rejoicing is based upon the certainty of the promises of one whose word will never fail.

Reasons for rejoicing (3:15-17)

Clear reasons are now given for the call to rejoice referred to in verse 14. This is the biblical way. A call from God to do something is invariably preceded or followed by a series of reasons for doing so. Unlike the inane exhortations of so much modern evangelicalism, true biblical Christianity is characterized by clearly articulated reasons and incentives for doing what it is called upon to do. Just as there are reasons to believe, so there are reasons to rejoice. Faith must never be reduced to mere believism, or faith in faith. In seeking to raise the tone of our worship or service we must not succumb to the temptation to employ pseudo-psychological techniques to acquire that which we desire.

The great overall reason for rejoicing here is that the things which God in his kindness has promised are *as good as done*. And that is really the point that has to be remembered. He has not yet accomplished what he has promised. The people have still to go into exile; there is still much suffering that will have to be endured. Full participation in the blessings that he will soon enunciate is still a distant reality to those who are called upon to rejoice in them. So then, how can they rejoice? On what basis is it possible? The specific grounds will soon be articulated, but the most essential reason for their rejoicing is that *he has promised.* The fact that he has promised means that these things are as good as done. Just as every other promise that God has ever made has been fulfilled, so too will these be; there can be no good reason to doubt it. So what does he promise? What are the specifics which compel them to rejoice?

1. The Lord has dealt with their most fundamental problem

The first explicit reason that Zephaniah offers for their rejoicing is that 'The LORD has taken away your punishment' (3:15). Although the immediate context justifies identifying those 'taken away' with the oppressive regime that had subjugated Israel, we would certainly be wrong if this is all that we did. Indeed, with good reason, both the NKJV and the ESV render the word 'punishment' in the plural ('judgements'). Ancient Israel's problems, like our own, are not simply, or even primarily, those that arise from external factors; they also arise from the sin that lives and threatens to rule in the human heart. It is this that has caused the invasions to come about in the first place; the wrath of God—whether it takes the form of an invading army sent to punish, or that accumulated outburst which awaits the impenitent at death or on the Day of Judgement (Romans 2:5)—is his response to sin's rebellion. Therefore to have this dealt with, to have it once and for all behind us, ought to be a great source of joy to the child of God.

In the New Testament, the apostle Paul expresses it like this: 'Therefore, since we have been justified through faith, we have peace with God through our Lord Jesus Christ, through whom we have gained access by faith into this grace in which we now stand. And we rejoice in the hope of the glory of God' (Romans 5:1-2). How wonderful this is—and to know it now, to have the assurance of it now! It is true that God will never be entirely satisfied with us until the full work of redemption is complete and, likewise, we should not be satisfied with ourselves. Nevertheless, it is a most significant cause for rejoicing to know that even now that work is as good as done already.

2. The Lord is against their enemies

A second reason for rejoicing is that 'He has turned back your enemy' (3:15). As has already been intimated, it must be remembered that this enemy was God's means of chastising his rebellious people. Neither the Assyrians who overthrew Israel in 722 BC nor the Babylonians who were destined to overthrow Judah in 586 BC had assailed God's people simply at their own instigation. As Matthew Poole has said, it is the Lord 'who kills and makes alive, acquits or condemns, and none can reverse the judgement'.[4] Those who made themselves the enemies of God's ancient people by invasion, subjugation and exile were nevertheless his unwitting instruments. But their time too would come. The Babylonians would be replaced by the Persians and, in due time, the Persians too would succumb to a conqueror of their own.

This was the Lord's answer to a later prophet's initial bewilderment when he too was faced with the mystery of God's dealings with his people. Even though he can take up and use an equally (or even more) wicked nation as his instrument against the wickedness of his own people, the time will come when they too will feel the smart of his just wrath against them (cf. Habakkuk 2:15–17). Here, then, is a further cause for rejoicing among the people of God. The wicked can do no more than God permits; moreover, they will never be permitted to triumph in their wickedness. God is always on the side of his people, and those who prove faithful will find that ultimate victory will be given into their hands (Deuteronomy 28:7).

3. The Lord is in their midst

The third reason for rejoicing is that 'The LORD, the King of Israel, is with you' (3:15). Surely there can be few blessings greater than the reality of the Lord's presence. Supreme happiness for the child of God is to know that he is in the midst of his people. Of course, the Lord never really forsakes them. His consistent promise to his people is that he will never do so (Deuteronomy 31:6, 8; Joshua 1:5; Hebrews 13:5). Sometimes, however, it is made to seem as if he is a long way off. This is especially (though not exclusively) so when we are consciously disobedient to him. As we have repeatedly seen in this prophecy, at such times God's anger is kindled against us. This is somewhat inevitable. The fact of the matter is that he can only be known and felt to be with his people in a positive sense when he is revered by them. Or, to use the very words suggested by the text, he can only be present as King. There can be no compromise in this. If we would have him with us, he must exert his kingly rights over us.

But just in case this should be thought a negative or a frightening thing, we are immediately informed of a series of welcome benefits of having such a King in the midst of his people.

Firstly, *all fear is banished:* 'Never again will you fear any harm.' No wonder they are expected to rejoice. When the Lord is among his people, neither disease from within nor invasion from without can meaningfully threaten them again. The reason is simple: he is with us. As Calvin says, to have God with us is to 'live under his guardianship and protection.'[5] Now who or what could meaningfully challenge the security provided by this 'King of kings'? At a much later date the eternal Son of God would offer similar assurances to his people, saying to them, 'I give them eternal life, and they shall never perish; no one can snatch them out of my hand. My Father, who has given them to me, is greater than all; no one can snatch them out of my Father's hand' (John 10:28–29). So, as these Old Testament people look to the future, they too can rejoice with confidence—God is in their midst and they have no need to fear.

Secondly, *all depression is lifted:*

On that day they will say to Jerusalem,
   'Do not fear, O Zion;
   do not let your hands hang limp'   (3:16).

The connection between this and the previous verse is obvious. There is a certain amount of repetition here. Not only is 'that day' kept firmly in focus, but also the theme of fear. Nevertheless, verse 16 is not simply a repetition of what has gone before. There is also development here. Fear is being connected with despair (cf. Isaiah 13:7). The picture presented is both graphic and immediately recognizable. It is a portrait of someone who has been reduced to utter despair. His hands, the instruments by which he normally does his work, are hanging limply by his side (cf. Hebrews 12:12; Isaiah 35:3). It is as if he has no energy left within him. He has been reduced to hopelessness; he doesn't have the heart to go on. This is a clear picture of what fear can do to us. We can, as we say, become 'paralysed with fear'. As the seventeenth-century Puritan George Hutcheson correctly observes, 'Faithless fainting, fear, and idleness are usual companions, which feed and entertain one another. Fear weakens the hands for duty, and idleness feeds discouragement yet more ...'[6]

But the whole point of this statement here is to remind the people of God that there is no reason why this condition should remain true of them. On 'that day' all the causes of their fearful and depressive anxiety will be removed. Indeed, the expectation of such a day should have the opposite effect; a new vigour should characterize both their countenance and their conduct. This should be especially so when they realize that 'On that day *they will say* to Jerusalem, "Do not fear, O Zion; do not let your hands hang limp' (emphasis added). Now the question is: who will say such things to the inhabitants of this city? The answer seems to be that their deliverance has become common knowledge; it is said by everyone (3:9-10). Such is the contrast between their former and present state that the whole world will join in the general approbation of the arrival of their longed-for peace and security. That day will throw off all discouragements. The prospect of this has important consequences even for their immediate situation. It is certainly not a time for selfish indulgence, and the next clause tells us why.

Thirdly, *omnipotence is on their side*. The verse begins, 'The Lord your God is with you' (3:17). Once again, this opening sounds very familiar (see 3:15). But even here something very special is immediately added. It is that this God is most definitely theirs ('your God'). This wonderful assurance is then immediately followed by another: 'He is mighty to save.' Differences exist among modern translators and commentators over the way the Hebrew word *gibbôr* should be rendered. Most prefer some variation of the NIV rendering—e.g., 'the Mighty One' (NKJV) or 'a mighty one' (ASV; ESV); others prefer the equally acceptable, though more dramatically descriptive, 'warrior' (RSV; NEB), or even 'a mighty hero' (Palmer Robertson). It is interesting to note that Palmer Robertson also identifies this designation with the 'mighty God' of Isaiah's Messianic prophecy (Isaiah 9:6).[7] What all are agreed upon, however, is that this person possesses formidable power. Not only is he 'mighty', but 'mighty *to save*'. In some versions this is even more definitely expressed: he is the one who *'will save'* (AV, ASV, NKJV) or who 'gives victory' (RSV); in another version he is 'a victorious warrior' (JB). The certainty of his victory is because of who he is. In the book of Deuteronomy he is described as the 'God of gods and Lord of lords, the great God, mighty and awesome' (Deuteronomy 10:17). None can withstand this kind of being.

We are immediately reminded of the New Testament and similar convictions that are found on the lips of the apostle Paul. Writing to the Christians in Rome, he reaches what must be, even by his standards, the most sublime heights of confidence when he says:

> If God is for us, who can be against us? He who did not spare his own Son, but gave him up for us all—how will he not also, along with him, graciously give us all things? Who will bring any charge against those whom God has chosen? It is God who justifies. Who is he that condemns? Christ Jesus, who died—more than that, who was raised to life—is at the right hand of God and is also interceding for us. Who shall separate us from the love of Christ? Shall trouble or hardship or persecution or famine or nakedness or danger or sword? As it is written:
>
> 'For your sake we face death all day long;
>   we are considered as sheep to be slaughtered.'
>
> No, in all these things we are more than conquerors through him who loved us. For I am convinced that neither death nor life, neither angels nor demons, neither the present nor the future, nor any powers, neither height nor depth, nor anything else in all creation, will be able to separate us from the love of God that is in Christ Jesus our Lord   (Romans 8:31–39).

Here, then, is another consequence of having God with us. No matter what the immediate circumstances might hold, here is another sure reason for the child of God to rejoice. God is present in all our circumstances. Moreover, he is present in power. And what power this is! Quite rightly, George Hutcheson says that the church may 'reckon her strength by what is in him'.[8] It is the arm of omnipotence that reaches out on behalf of his people. It is a power that saves: '... he will save his people from their sins' (Matthew 1:21). But there is more.

4. The Lord assures them of the depth of his love

The fourth reason for rejoicing is that the Lord loves them (3:17)—and with such a love! Indeed, God is now seen to be doing that which he had previously exhorted his people to do. He is exalting, delighting, rejoicing and singing—*over them!* Palmer Robertson calls this verse 'the John 3:16 of the Old Testament'[9] and it is not difficult to see why he does so. In three simple but stunning ways the prophet reminds the people of the great experiential love that awaits these people.

Firstly, the prophet says that 'He will take great delight in you.' These words begin to express the depth of his love for his people. It is not just that they will learn to delight in their gracious Lord, but that he will delight in them. Indeed, there is to be a mutual joy and rejoicing in their love for each other. This is truly astounding. As Palmer Robertson comments, 'That Almighty God should derive delight from his own creation is significant in itself. But that the Holy One should experience ecstasy over the sinner is incomprehensible.'[10]

This delight is grounded in the kind of God he is; he is a God of mercy (Micah 7:18). Few things give him as much pleasure as being able to show kindness to his people. He delights to take

on the role of the father whose ever-loving arms embrace the
returning prodigal (Luke 15:11–32). He is like the once-jilted lover
who now delights in taking the object of his love for his bride
(Isaiah 62:5; cf. 65:19). Although his delight in them can be as
vocal as theirs should be for him (3:14), here it is one of stillness
and quiet. This is, after all, a solemn day; judgement has fallen.
But, as David Baker reminds us, 'The battle cry on the day of
judgement (1:14) will be replaced by the poignant hush of the
reuniting of two lovers.'[11]

Secondly, the prophet says that 'He will quiet you with his
love.' It is possible to translate this clause in different ways.
Many prefer to see God as the one who is 'quiet' (or who 'rests')
in his love for his people: 'he will rest in his love' (AV), or 'he will
be silent in his love' (AV margin.). They see here the Warrior,
'mighty to save', now resting in the satisfaction of his victory and
the loving relationship that exists between him and his people.
The war is over, and a new people acknowledge his rule and
trust his name (cf. 3:12). In other words, this is a picture of great
contentment in the heart of God over what he has achieved on
behalf of his people.

If such language is thought excessive, Palmer Robertson first
reminds us that 'God is love' (1 John 4:8), and then continues
with the following observation: 'If a human being with all the
limitations of his nature may revel in the purity of essential love
in short, snatched moments, then certainly the Almighty himself
may reach even greater depths of love and sustain these depths
without restriction of time.'[12]

Calvin too sides with those who translate these words as an
expression of God's self-contented love, but he also justifies
them in terms of divine condescension and accommodation. He

writes, 'He [God] assumes the person of a mortal man, because, unless He stammers in this manner, He cannot sufficiently show how much He loves us. *Thy God will therefore be quiet in His love, i.e.* this will be the greatest delight of thy God, this His chief pleasure, when He shall cherish thee. As a man caresses his dearest wife, so will God then quietly repose in thy love.'[13]

Both the NIV and the NKJV, however, see this as an act of God towards his people. He will quiet 'you'—that is, 'Jerusalem', 'Zion', 'Israel', the people of God. In his translation, Moffatt simply says that the Lord 'renews his love'. After all they have been through, he will quiet them with tokens of his love. He will, in New Testament terms, 'shed his love abroad in our hearts' (Romans 5:5)—a love that is beyond all human comprehension.

Finally, the prophet says, 'He will rejoice over you with singing.' Having exhorted them to rejoice, it is now time for God to rejoice over them. Again the picture of a father's response to a 'prodigal son' readily comes to mind (Luke 15:22–24). Or perhaps these words suggest the love of a man for his wife. Certainly, this is how Calvin views them—and he anticipates trouble in doing so. He wonders about the possibility of demeaning God's glory by the use of such comparisons. Perhaps the fact that such scruples rarely even occur to us says more than we might wish to consider!

Nevertheless, the sixteenth-century Reformer not only reminds his readers that God has himself stooped to employ such analogies, but that it is vitally necessary for our sakes that he should do so. He writes, 'It is not without reason that God labours so much to persuade us of his love, because we are not only prone by nature to unbelief, but exposed to the deceits of Satan, and are also inconstant and easily drawn away from his word: hence it is that he assumes the character of man. We must, at the same time, observe what I have before stated— that whatever is calculated to set forth the love of God, does not derogate from his glory; for his chief glory is that vast and ineffable goodness by which he has once embraced us, and which he will show us to the end.'[14]

Without doubt this is true. It simply remains for the recipients of such love to bow before him in awe and wonder. With Matthew Henry we say, 'O the condescensions of divine grace! The great God not only loves his saints, but he loves to love them, is pleased that he has pitched upon these objects of his love.'[15]

With all the words of this section, the prophet seems mindful of the promise God had made long ago to his people when they found themselves in what seemed to be uncertain times. On the brink of the promised land, and having reminded them of the dangerous realities of apostasy, Moses goes on to spell out God's response to their subsequent repentance. He says, 'The LORD will again *delight in you* and make you prosperous, *just as he delighted in your fathers*, if you obey the LORD your God and keep his commands and decrees that are written in this Book of the Law and turn to the LORD your God with all your heart and with all your soul' (Deuteronomy 30:9-10). This is indeed good news. Even on the brink of judgement, promises of love and mercy are held out to a needy people. And those promises will still be in place even when these people find themselves in exile.

> Here is love, vast as the ocean
> Lovingkindness as the flood,
> When the Prince of life, our ransom,
> Shed for us his precious blood.

Who his love will not remember?
Who can cease to sing his praise?
He can never be forgotten
Throughout heaven's eternal days.

On the Mount of Crucifixion
Fountains opened deep and wide;
Through the floodgates of God's mercy
Flowed a vast and gracious tide.
Grace and love, like mighty rivers,
Poured incessant from above,
And heaven's peace and perfect justice
Kissed a guilty world in love

William Rees (1802–83)
translated by William Edwards (1848–1929).

Points to ponder

There can be no doubt that these words have a partial fulfilment in the restoration of the ancient people of God to Israel during the reign of Cyrus (Ezra 1:1–4). They also find their ultimate fulfilment (as do all the words of this prophecy) in the great Day of Judgement and the establishment of 'a new heavens and a new earth'. But they are words which contain great significance for these gospel days too. For these also should be days of rejoicing for all those who have tasted that the Lord is good in the bestowal of the wonders of his salvation.

1. We too know what it is to have the punishment for our sins taken away.

God himself has taken them away. He has done this through the sacrificial death of his Son. In a single stroke, once and for ever, through the death of Jesus Christ upon the cross, he has put away the cause of his just wrath against us. Sin has now been dealt with; the threat of its penalty has been removed from us 'as far as the east is from the west' (Psalm 103:12). Never again will their sins be counted against those who repent and believe the gospel (Psalm 32:1–2; Romans 4:8; 2 Corinthians 5:17–19). This is a genuine cause for rejoicing even now, before death and eternity dawn.

2. We too know what it is to have the Lord on our side against our enemies.

Who are our enemies? They are the world, the flesh and the devil. When we speak of this unholy triad, we are thinking of that spirit of opposition to God which, since man's original fall in the Garden of Eden, enslaves the hearts of the unregenerate. Satan ever seeks to exploit their sad condition by promoting the twin evils of pride and covetousness in their minds. However, the dominance of this spirit has been broken by the regenerating power of the Holy Spirit in those who have been brought to faith in Jesus Christ. Their former friends are now their enemies. In place of quiet submission, the newborn Christian finds himself at war with the world, the flesh and the devil. In this fight he is not alone. God is on his side; the enemies that the Christian fights are his Lord's enemies too. Indeed, they are our enemies because they are first his. Moreover, the final outcome of this battle is not in doubt; omnipotence shall prevail. This too is a source of joyful encouragement to the child of God.

3. We too know what it is to have a felt sense of God's love in our hearts.

This is not just an objective fact, but an experiential reality (cf. Romans 5:5). There is nothing to be compared with this blessing and the assurance that it brings. In its strength we are able to draw near to God with assurance, knowing that we are acceptable to him. The words 'Abba Father' fall confidently from our lips in prayer; fear and despondency are expelled by its presence, and we enjoy a holy boldness before God and men. What is more, this is not just something reserved for the future; in wonderfully various degrees of intensity, the assurance of this love is known and felt *now*. And whatever is experienced now, this is just a foretaste of greater blessings yet to come. No wonder the Christian is expected to 'Rejoice in the Lord always' (Philippians 4:4).

10

God will restore blessedness
to his people

Please read Zephaniah 3:18–20

It might at first glance seem somewhat strange that this prophecy does not simply close on the high note of the preceding verses. The people of God had been called upon to rejoice in all the glorious blessings that awaited them. Not least among these were the promises of the Lord's commitment to their welfare, the certainty of their eventual triumph and the blessings of his love. However, instead of just leaving it at that, a further series of statements appear which actually seem to add very little to what has already been said. Indeed, the words that conclude this prophecy are to a large extent a restatement of the promises that have already been made.

Moreover, although these are encouraging in their own right, they certainly cannot be said even to come close to matching the grandeur of those that have already been uttered. Therefore, the most natural question to ask is: why are these words added at all? Perhaps the answer is to be found in the simple observation that, for those living in Zephaniah's day, the fulfilment of these promises was still a long way off. Their trial of faith was still destined to take them down a long and difficult road before they would finally emerge into the sunshine of repatriation.

The Lord's reminders

In other words, we must always remember that the first thing that awaited these people was judgement. As Moses and the prophets had testified, this nation would be dispersed among the nations of the world, and refined in the fires of affliction. The ten tribes of Israel had already been carried away; Judah was to follow. Nothing would be more important to them during their exile than that they should be reminded, and repeatedly reminded, that something far better was still to come. This is not, as some would allege, merely the promise of 'pie in the sky when you die'. As we shall see, these promises are based on something solid and certain; they are based on the sure Word of God. Nevertheless, reminders, even double reminders, would be constantly needed if the people of God were to see beyond the immediacy of their present difficult circumstances to that which lies beyond the mountains ranged in front of them. This is a familiar tactic employed by biblical writers and is as necessary for those who await the dawn of a new heaven and a new earth as it was for the people of Zion longing for restoration to their promised land.

Therefore, as this particular prophecy draws to a close, there is a final undergirding of those promises that point to an ultimate victory. There would be times when the people would be reduced to misery, oppression and utter disgrace, but the

Warrior-King is on the horizon. He will raise them up again, and not merely to what they were before, but to something far greater and far better. They must hang on to these promises. A new day will dawn.

As C. F. Keil summarizes, 'In order, therefore, to offer to the pious a firm consolation of hope in the period of suffering that awaited them, and one on which their faith could rest in the midst of tribulation, Zephaniah mentions in conclusion the gathering together of all who pine in misery at a distance from Zion, and who are scattered far and wide, to assure even these of their future participation in the promised salvation.'[1]

The Lord's determination
And so we turn to the words of the text. We begin with three general observations. Each of these has been made before but, when brought together as they are in these concluding verses, they add up to a most powerful statement about the Lord's determination to effect all that he has promised. It is vitally important to remember that there lurks behind every promise that Scripture makes the implacable will of a determined Sovereign. This is again highlighted by the use of words 'I will' (3:18-20), 'at that time' (3:19-20) and 'says the LORD' (3:20).

1. The persistence of the 'I wills'
No one should ever doubt the Lord's determination to bring to pass every detail of his good and sovereign will. What he says, he will do. And *he* will do it. This God is not the sort who will follow the script vainly held out to him by Deist scriptwriters. He is no 'hands-off' deity—the kind who is supposed to have made the world much as a watchmaker might make a timepiece, wind it up and then finally leave it to its own inner workings. The God of the Bible is constantly involved in the work of his

hands. This fact is emphasized throughout this prophecy where, in the first person, God announces his own involvement with the things that will yet be brought to pass, and he repeatedly does so using the words, 'I will'. In these three short chapters this emphasis appears no less than twenty-one times in our English translations. He not only speaks, but he speaks as one who is determined to act.

Most of these 'I wills' underscore that which he is determined to do *in judgement*. As we have already seen, he is the one who will 'sweep away everything': men, animals, birds and even fish (1:1–3). It is he who will 'stretch out [his] hand' against his own people (1:4). Idolatry is the cause (1:5); both leaders and those who follow them will be tracked down and punished (1:6–7, 12). And when he finds them, there will be no mercy: distress and anguish, trouble and ruin, darkness and gloom will overtake them. They will look around to see who it is that has overwhelmed them, and they will see the one who has said, 'I will' (1:15–17). Those living among the surrounding nations who have likewise lived in idolatry and have oppressed the people of God will discover that this same God is against them too (2:5). Moreover, should anyone dare to imagine that the verdict being pronounced against them can be challenged, this awesome Judge will himself rise up to testify against them (3:8). These 'I wills' are formidable declarations from the mouth of the living God who comes to exercise judgements.

But not only will he intervene in judgement; he will also come *in mercy*. He has great love for his people and he is equally determined to restore to them the prosperity they once knew. This will involve restoring purity to their lips (3:9), removing pride from their midst (3:11) and filling their horizons with those glorious spiritual virtues of meekness, humility and faith (3:12).

All this he promises to do: 'I will'. And he has not finished. If we are to include the 'when I restore your fortunes' among them (and surely we must), the 'I wills' appear no less than seven times in these last three verses alone. It is as if the Lord is redoubling his efforts to assure his faithful people that all that has been done will be fulfilled.

2. The assurance of 'at that time'

The assurance of this same determination is to be found when we are seeking an answer to the question: when will these promises be fulfilled? No less than three times in two verses, the Lord assures them that these promises will be brought to pass 'at that time' (3:19–20)—that is, at the same time that he does all the other things that are mentioned in these verses. This immediately suggests two things: firstly, that God has a purpose and that it will certainly be accomplished. His sovereignty shines through once again.

There is, according to Calvin, a 'fixed time of deliverance'; there is 'a predetermined time'.[2] Once spotted, this is something that continually leaps out at us throughout the Scriptures. In its pages we are constantly, and reassuringly, brought face-to-face with the combination of a 'set purpose' (Acts 2:23) and an 'appointed' time (Hebrews 9:27, NKJV), or a 'fulness of time' (Galatians 4:4, ESV). No matter how bad things may seem to be from a human perspective, there is nothing haphazard about the ways of God: 'He has made everything beautiful in its time' (Eccles. 3:11). This, again, should constantly inspire the believing heart with confidence.

But, secondly, Calvin is equally keen that we should recognize another lesson taught by the reality of God's sovereignty; it should teach us to be patient. 'At that time' is *his* time, not ours. Calvin writes, 'Our prophet then holds the faithful here somewhat in suspense, that they might continue in their watchtower, and patiently wait for God's help; for we know how great is our haste, and how we run headlong when we hope for anything; but this celerity [swiftness], according to the old proverb, is often to delay us. Since, then, men are always carried away by a certain heat, or by too much impetuosity, to lay hold on what may happen, the Prophet here lays a restraint, and intimates that God has his own seasons to fulfil what he has promised, that he will not do so soon, nor according to the will of men, but when the suitable times shall come. And this time is that which he has appointed, not what we desire.'[3]

So, then, from these two observations, we catch a glimpse of the reassurances that the Bible's teaching on the sovereignty of God places before believing people. This teaching is not something to be feared; still less is it something to be opposed. Its truth is set before God's people in order that they might face the trials of the present and the uncertainties of the future with a patient reliance upon his infallible Word.

3. The final certainty of 'says the Lord'
And it is that infallible Word that comes clearly into view with our last general observation and the final words of this book. The prophecy ends with the words, 'says the LORD'. These are the words that most commonly fall from the lips of the Old Testament prophets. They were not only meant to reassure the people of the identity of the true author of the words spoken, but of the trustworthiness of the content of the messages themselves. This was the final confirmation that all that had been said would come to pass. In the Bible, the Word of God is always associated with the truth of God (John 17:17; cf. Isaiah 8:20). It is always associated with something powerful (Genesis

1:3) and certain (Isaiah 55:11). Jesus Christ himself not only speaks it, but has absolute confidence in it: it is the final word (Matthew 4:4, 6–7) and cannot be broken (John 10:35).

Therefore, although the days may be long and hard before the promises of God are fulfilled, the mere passing of time must not be allowed to undermine the faith of God's people. Remember, 'With the Lord a day is like a thousand years, and a thousand years are like a day' (2 Peter 3:8). The Lord of the Universe has given his word, and he will keep all his promises. As Jesus Christ said, 'Heaven and earth will pass away, but my words will never pass away' (Matthew 24:35).

The Lord's promises
Having completed our three general observations, we can now turn to the promises themselves. What is it that God promises to do for his people? What incentive to perseverance does he set before them that they might be encouraged to press on? In a nutshell, he repeats his promise to restore a state of blessedness to his people. He sets this out in a number of ways.

1. He will remove their sorrows (3:18)
The first thing that the Lord does is to assure the people that he will remove the main cause of their sorrow. Some translations follow the Septuagint in linking verse 18 with the immediately preceding verse. But the sombre opening of this verse suggests that a new thought is in view, and it is. With God himself once more immediately addressing the faithful, the focus is again on the felt deprivations that will accompany the judgement.

First among them is a sense of loss: 'The sorrows for the appointed feasts I will remove from you.' As a people, they have been dispersed ('scattered', 3:19) among the nations, with all that this would mean in terms of a denial of access to the religious festivals that the best of former generations had once held so dear. It is to their credit that this is now among their foremost concerns.

As the seventeenth-century commentator Matthew Henry puts it, 'The city is ruined, and the palaces are demolished; trade is at an end, and the administration of public justice; but all these are nothing to them in comparison with the desolations of the sanctuary, the destruction of the temple and the altar, to attend on which, in solemn feasts, all Israel used to come together three times a year. It is for those sacred solemn assemblies that they are sorrowful.'[4]

Their sorrows are aggravated by an accompanying sense of burden and reproach: '... they are a burden and a reproach to you.' In the first place, their lack of access to 'the appointed feasts' would be a constant reminder of the reasons for their exile. Successive generations had been disobedient to the covenant that the Lord had established with them. They had neglected and abused their ritual obligations. Now, following judgement and exile to a strange land, their very distance from the place where those rituals were once celebrated would bring the burden of their disgrace home to them. But, secondly, just living as a despised and disgraced people among their conquerors would be a further source of discomfort to them. They would undoubtedly suffer the taunts of their conquerors, something so movingly expressed by the composer of Psalm 137:

By the waters of Babylon we sat and wept
    when we remembered Zion.
There on the poplars
    we hung our harps,

for there our captors asked us for songs,
    our tormentors demanded songs of joy;
    they said, 'Sing us one of the songs of Zion!'

How can we sing the songs of the Lord
    while in a foreign land?
If I forget you, O Jerusalem,
    may my right hand forget its skill.
May my tongue cling to the roof of my mouth
    if I do not remember you,
    if I do not consider Jerusalem
        my highest joy.

But this sense of despair is set to change. A new day will dawn
and the process of dispersion will be reversed.

2. He will deal with their oppressors (3:19)

Not only would these people experience a sense of loss, but
they were under oppression. At the appointed time, God will
step in and lift the oppression. He will do so by dealing with
the oppressors themselves: 'At that time I will deal with all
who oppressed you.' This has already been assured (3:15) but,
under the torments of the oppression itself, the temptation to
despair must have been very strong. This repetition is therefore
intended to counter that tendency. There is, however, an
additional factor here. The blessings of 'that time' will not be
confined to the removal of oppressors. There is to be a gathering
too.

What immediately follows is an almost exact repetition of
Micah 4:6. The Lord says, 'I will rescue the lame and gather
those who have been scattered.' This is almost certainly intended
to reinforce the truth that no condition—not even lameness—

will hinder God's rescue of his people and their restoration to the promised land. The gathering implies more than a simple restoration to the land. As Palmer Robertson says, 'They shall be assembled as a reconstituted community of God's people.'[5] The law had threatened banishment, but there were promises of restoration too (Deuteronomy 30:1,4).

3. He will renovate their reputation (3:19–20)

In addition to this, there is the promise of a change in the way in which these people will be viewed by those around them. No longer will they be the objects of reproach. Instead they will be objects of praise and honour: 'I will give them praise and honour in every land where they were put to shame.' This statement harks back to the promise made in Deuteronomy 26:19: 'He has declared that he will set you in praise, fame and honour high above all the nations he has made and that you will be a people holy to the LORD your God, as he promised.' Outside the books of Deuteronomy and Zephaniah, this precise combination of 'praise and honour' (literally, 'praise and a name') is to be found only in Jeremiah 13:11. This observation may well point to the book of Deuteronomy being a source for both prophets. Its main thought is that, as a result of what has happened to them, the once-despised people of God now find themselves the objects of awe and respect from the surrounding nations. This sudden elevation has nothing to do with any supposed merit in themselves. It is entirely due to the activity of God.

This gathering and honouring are reiterated, and their application expanded, in the closing verse of this prophecy. The emphasis is still upon that which will happen 'at that time'—that is, on the day appointed for judgement and restoration. Three things are stressed.

Firstly, 'I will gather you.' As was said before, this simple reiteration of the statement made in the previous verse is probably in order to underline the fact that this gathering will really happen. According to Calvin, when the Jews were in exile they were like people who had been cast into a grave;[6] the last thing in the world that they could imagine is that they would ever be delivered. Nevertheless, the promise, though difficult to believe, would be fulfilled.

Secondly, 'At that time I will bring you home.' This is a particularly encouraging touch. Not only are the remnant to be 'gathered', but brought 'home'. What else could this possibly suggest but a restoration to Jerusalem, with all the joys promised by that designation?

Thirdly, although the words are not specifically used again, 'at that time' is clearly envisaged. This time it is to reiterate what had been said in the previous verse: 'I will give you honour and praise among all the peoples ...' There is no need to see in the reverse order of 'honour and praise' anything more than poetic variation. The most important thing to notice is the widening expanse of those from whom they will receive this acknowledgement. Not only will this acknowledgement be found 'in every land where they were put to shame', but 'among all the peoples of the earth'.

4. He will restore their fortunes (3:20)

The final clause of this prophecy provides a general answer to the question: when will all that has been prophesied in this book take place? When will 'that day' which will bring both judgement and restoration arrive? When will 'honour and praise' be lavished upon the people of God 'among all the peoples of the earth'? The answer supplied by most English translations is either 'when

I restore your fortunes' (NIV) or 'when I return your captives' (NKJV); either translation is possible.

In favour of the latter rendering, 'when I return your captives', is the thought that it most naturally suits the restoration of the Jews from exile that took place during the reign of King Cyrus II of Persia in 539 BC Nevertheless, even though this event would be included, it does seem that something on a far grander scale is ultimately in view. This bigger picture is suggested by two things: firstly, it is doubtful whether the promise to give Israel honour 'among all the peoples of the earth' was fulfilled at the time of the restoration under Cyrus. Secondly, the words that immediately follow, and which also form part of the promise, speak of its details being fulfilled 'before your very eyes'. Although a somewhat problematic statement, it seems reasonable to conclude with Palmer Robertson that 'Neither Zephaniah's contemporaries nor those who lived to see the restoration of Israel to Palestine experienced all that the prophet promised.'[7]

Furthermore, given the fact that the larger context of this passage also refers to the judgement of the whole earth (1:2–3,18; 3:8), the salvation of pagan nations (3:9–10) and the state of complete triumph enjoyed by those restored (3:11–17), it is difficult to resist the conclusion that an ultimate fulfilment of this prophecy can only be realized at the glorious return of Jesus Christ and the rejuvenation of the entire universe.

Indeed, this is the conclusion to which Palmer Robertson (along with many others) is also drawn. He writes, 'The imagery of Israel's possession of Palestine actually builds on the picture of paradise restored. The prophet had spoken in terms reminiscent of the idyllic situation of paradise (3:13).

The original promise of the land to the first father of Israel, as well as the assurance of a multiplied seed, actually reflects the original creation mandate concerning humanity's responsibility to multiply, fill the earth, and subdue it (Genesis 1:28). In microcosmic fashion, the possession of the land by the descendants of Abraham depicted the manner in which God would complete his program for the redemption of the earth. *When I return your* [i.e., Israel's] *captivity* anticipates the rejuvenation of the world. For it actually was the "cosmos" that Abraham and his seed were promised (Romans 4:13).'[8]

Therefore, those final reassuring words, 'says the LORD', take us back to where this entire prophecy began (1:1). But they do so with a difference. The initial stages of Zephaniah's message contained almost nothing but doom and disaster. Nevertheless, another side of what will transpire on 'the Day of the Lord' is also allowed to emerge from this book. While it is true that 'that day' will be one of inexplicable horror to those who have opposed God and his covenant, it will also be one that will usher in an unparalleled and unsurpassable state of everlasting blessedness for the people of God. It will be a glorious day of bodily resurrection, perfect freedom from all the debilitating effects of sin and death, complete harmony throughout a rejuvenated universe and, the greatest prize of all, Christlikeness: 'Dear friends, now we are children of God, and what we will be has not yet been made known. But we know that when he appears, we shall be like him, for we shall see him as he is' (1 John 3:2).

In another place, the apostle John goes on to sum up this glorious blessing in these words: 'Then I saw a new heaven and a new earth, for the first heaven and the first earth had passed away, and there was no longer any sea. I saw the Holy City, the new Jerusalem, coming down out of heaven from God, prepared as a bride beautifully dressed for her husband. And I heard a loud voice from the throne saying, "Now the dwelling of God is with men, and he will live with them. They will be his people, and God himself will be with them and be their God. He will wipe every tear from their eyes. There will be no more death or mourning or crying or pain, for the old order of things has passed away"' (Revelation 21:1–4).

This is what awaits the people of God. This is what is promised; this is what shall be fulfilled. The Lord, in his infallible Word, says so.

Points to ponder
The fact that God has made something (not all) of his sovereign will known should be a source of tremendous encouragement to the people of God. In the passage of Scripture that we have just considered, by setting out a series of reminders concerning the blessedness that awaits his people, he shows that he understands us (Psalm 103:14) and is willing to accommodate himself to our weaknesses. In doing so, he gladdens our hearts, replenishes our courage and excites our faith.

1. It means that there are certain things for which we can pray, knowing that we are asking for that which is consistent with God's sovereign will.
In one of the best definitions of prayer ever given, John Bunyan writes, 'Prayer is a sincere, sensible, affectionate pouring out of the heart or soul to God, through Christ, in the strength and assistance of the Holy Spirit, *for such things as God has promised, or according to his Word,* for the good of the church, with submission in faith to the will of God.'9

The emphasis to which I have drawn attention in this definition reminds us of the importance of paying close attention to the promises of God. When our prayers are consistent with God's revealed will, we can venture boldly into his presence confident that his will shall be done. We are not only to 'think God's thoughts after him' (as Augustine says), but pray God's thoughts after him.

2. It means that there are certain things that we can be sure will happen, because God himself has declared that they shall come to pass.
The key to the Christian life is that 'We live by faith, not by sight.' But what does this actually mean? It means that in the midst of the battles that rage within us, and around us, we must choose to trust and follow as true that which God has revealed in his Word. Not only is this attitude taught by the Word itself (Matthew 4:4), but it makes very good sense. After all, in order to be God, he must *know* better than anyone else, be more *powerful* than anyone else and be more *determined* than we can ever imagine.

3. It means that there are certain things to which we can look forward, chief among them being the blessedness of 'paradise regained'.
Scripture clearly reveals that there will come a day when Jesus Christ will suddenly, and physically, return to the world that he has made. On that occasion it will not be a matter of 'veiled in flesh the Godhead see'; instead, there will be a full and open manifestation of his glory. In accordance with his many promises, he will judge the living and the dead and establish 'a new heaven and a new earth, the home of righteousness' (2 Peter 3:13). Paradise will be regained, but better than it ever was under the old order. Christ will be its King and, without even the

possibility of sin intruding, his people will for ever live in glad and glorious service of the one who 'loved us and gave himself for us'. This is the sure and certain hope that is set before us.

> Jesus, immortal King, go on;
> The glorious day will soon be won;
> Thine enemies prepare to flee,
> And leave the conquered world to thee.
>
> Gird on thy sword, victorious Chief!
> The captive sinner's sole relief;
> Cast the usurper from his throne,
> And make the universe thine own.
>
> Then shall contending nations rest,
> For love shall reign in every breast;
> Weapons, for war designed, shall cease,
> Or then be implements of peace.
>
> Thy footsteps, Lord, with joy we trace,
> And mark the conquests of thy grace;
> Finish the work thou hast begun,
> And let thy will on earth be done.
>
> Hark! how the hosts triumphant sing,
> 'The Lord Omnipotent is King!'
> Let all the saints rejoice at this,
> The kingdoms of the world are his!
>
> Thomas Kelly (1769–1855).

Notes

Introduction

1 W. Kuhrt, *Interpreting the Bible* (London: Grace Publications, 1991).

2 R. Mayhue, *How to Interpret the Bible* (Ross-shire: Christian Focus Publications, 1997).

3 G. D. Fee & D. Stuart, *How to Read the Bible for All its Worth* (Grand Rapids: Zondervan, 1993).

4 L. Berkhof, *Principles of Biblical Interpretation* (Grand Rapids: Baker Book House, 1950).

5 P. Fairbairn, *The Interpretation of Prophecy* (London: Banner of Truth Trust, 1964 [first published 1865]).

6 B. Milne, *Know the Truth: A Handbook of Christian Belief* (Leicester: Inter-Varsity Press, 1998), pp. 59–62.

7 *Ibid.*, p. 62.

8   Fee & Stuart, *How to Read the Bible for All its Worth,* p. 166.

9   Berkhof, *Principles of Biblical Interpretation,* p. 150.

10 D. Bonhoeffer, *The Cost of Discipleship* (London: SCM, 1963).

Chapter 1 — The man, the message, the season

1   R. Bolt, *A Man for All Seasons* (Oxford: Heinemann Educational Books, 1970).

2   See the 'Historical background' section in the introduction (pp. 14–17).

3   See the section in the introduction on 'The timing of Zephaniah's prophecy' (pp. 22–3).

Chapter 2 — God will judge his world

1   J. H. Charlesworth (ed.), *The Ascension of Isaiah* in *The Old Testament Pseudepigrapha* (New York: Doubleday, 1985), vol. 2, pp. 165–6.

2   See the section in the introduction on 'Understanding prophecy' (pp. 19–21).

Chapter 3 — God will judge his people

1   O. Palmer Robertson, *The Books of Nahum, Habakkuk, and Zephaniah* (Grand Rapids: Eerdmans, 1986), p. 263.

2   J. Edwards, *The History of Redemption* (Edinburgh: Thomas Nelson, 1841), p. 166.

3   For further information about 'Molech' and the practice of sacrificing children see J. A. Thomson's contribution in *The Illustrated Bible Dictionary* (Leicester: IVP, 1980), vol. 2, p. 1,018.

4   M. Poole, *A Commentary on the Bible* (London: Banner of Truth Trust, 1962), vol. 2, p. 977.

5   J. Calvin, *Calvin's Commentaries* (Grand Rapids: Baker Book House, 1979), vol. 15 (*Minor Prophets*, vol. 4), pp. 209–10.

6   C. F. Keil. & K. Delitzsch, *Commentary on the Old Testament* (Massachusetts: Hendrickson, 1989), vol. 10, p. 132.

7   M. Henry, *Commentary on the Whole Bible* (Massachusetts: Hendrickson, 1991), vol. 4, p. 1,083.

8   D. W. Baker, *Nahum, Habakkuk, Zephaniah* (Leicester: IVP, 1988), p. 99.

Chapter 4—The great Day of the Lord

1   Poole, *A Commentary on the Bible*, vol. 2, p. 978.

Chapter 5 — God's judgement is mixed with mercy

1   J. Edwards, *Works* (Edinburgh: Banner of Truth Trust, 1974), vol. 2, pp. 7–12.

2   I. H. Murray, *Jonathan Edwards* (Edinburgh: Banner of Truth Trust, 1987), pp. 168–70.

3   J. Tracy, *The Great Awakening* (Edinburgh: Banner of Truth Trust, 1976), p. 216.

4   Henry, *Commentary*, vol. 4, p. 1,084.

5   Palmer Robertson, *The Books of Nahum, Habakkuk, and Zephaniah*, pp. 289–90.

6   Ibid., p. 291.

7 Edwards, *Works,* vol. 2, p. 10.

8 *Ibid.,* p. 10.

9 *Ibid.,* p. 11.

10 G. Hutcheson, *Exposition of the Minor Prophets* (Michigan: Sovereign Grace Publishers, 1962), p. 300.

Chapter 6 — God's judgement will extend to the nations

1 R. C. Sproul, J. Gerstner, A. Lindsley, *Classical Apologetics* (Michigan: Zondervan, 1984), p. 27.

2 J. Calvin, *Calvin's Commentaries,* vol. 5 (*Psalms,* vol. 3), p. 391.

3 Poole, *A Commentary on the Bible,* vol. 2, p. 979.

4 *Ibid.*

5 Henry, *Commentary,* vol. 4, pp. 1,086–7.

6 See Xenophon, *Anabasis,* 3.4.8–12.

7 Palmer Robertson, *The Books of Nahum, Habakkuk, and Zephaniah,* p. 313.

Chapter 7 — God's judgement will embrace Jerusalem

1 Calvin, *Calvin's Commentaries,* vol. 15, p. 264.

2 Palmer Robertson, *The Books of Nahum, Habakkuk, and Zephaniah,* p. 319.

3 Baker, *Nahum, Habakkuk, Zephaniah,* p. 112.

4 *Ibid.,* p. 112.

5 Calvin, *Calvin's Commentaries,* vol. 15, p. 273.

6 Hutcheson, *Exposition of the Minor Prophets,* p. 318.

7 Calvin, *Calvin's Commentaries,* vol. 15, p. 276.

8 Hutcheson, *Exposition of the Minor Prophets,* pp. 319–20.

9 J. M. Boice, *Psalms: An Expositional Commentary* (Grand Rapids: Baker Books, 1996), vol. 2, p. 427.

Chapter 8 — God will restore hope to all his people

1 See R. V. G. Tasker's excellent article on 'Hope' in *The New Bible Dictionary,* ed. J. D. Douglas (London: Inter-Varsity Fellowship, 1965), pp. 535–6.

2 *Ibid.,* p. 535.

3 H. Hailey, *A Commentary on the Minor Prophets* (Grand Rapids: Baker Book House, 1972), p. 243.

4 *Ibid.,* p. 243.

5 T. Laetsch, *The Minor Prophets* (Saint Louis: Concordia Publishing House, 1956), p. 377.

6 D. W. Baker, *New Bible Commentary: Zephaniah* (Leicester: Inter-Varsity Press, 1994), p. 855.

7 Palmer Robertson, *The Books of Nahum, Habakkuk, and Zephaniah,* p. 331.

8 Edwards, *Works,* vol. 1, pp. 314–36.

9   Baker, *Nahum, Habakkuk, Zephaniah*, p. 117.

10 Tasker, 'Hope', *New Bible Dictionary*, p. 535.

Chapter 9 — God will restore rejoicing among his people

1   Palmer Robertson, *The Books of Nahum, Habakkuk, and Zephaniah*, p. 336.

2   Calvin, *Calvin's Commentaries*, vol. 15, p. 299.

3   A. Alexander, *Thoughts on Religious Experience* (London: Banner of Truth Trust, 1967), pp. 51–8.

4   Poole, *A Commentary on the Bible*, vol. 2, p. 982.

5   Calvin, *Calvin's Commentaries*, vol. 15, p. 301.

6   Hutcheson, *Exposition of the Minor Prophets*, p. 327.

7   Palmer Robertson, *The Books of Nahum, Habakkuk, and Zephaniah*, p. 338.

8   Hutcheson, *Exposition of the Minor Prophets*, p. 328.

9   Palmer Robertson, *The Books of Nahum, Habakkuk, and Zephaniah*, p. 339.

10 *Ibid.*, p. 340.

11 Baker, *Nahum, Habakkuk, Zephaniah*, p. 119.

12 Palmer Robertson, *The Books of Nahum, Habakkuk, and Zephaniah*, p. 341.

13 This quotation of Calvin is taken from the translation provided by Keil & Delitzsch in their *Commentary on the Old Testament*, vol. 10, p. 161.

14 Calvin, *Calvin's Commentaries,* vol. 15, p. 305.

15 Henry, *Commentary,* vol. 4, p. 1092.

Chapter 10 — God will restore blessedness to his people

1 Keil & Delitzsch, *Commentary on the Old Testament,* vol. 10, p. 162.

2 Calvin, *Calvin's Commentaries,* vol. 15, p. 307.

3 *Ibid.,* p. 307.

4 Henry, *Commentary,* vol. 4, p. 1092.

5 Palmer Robertson, *The Books of Nahum, Habakkuk, and Zephaniah,* p. 345.

6 Calvin, *Calvin's Commentaries,* vol. 15, p. 311.

7 Palmer Robertson, *The Books of Nahum, Habakkuk, and Zephaniah,* p. 346.

8 *Ibid.,* p. 346.

9 John Bunyan, *Prayer* (London: Banner of Truth Trust, 1965), p. 13.